1993

HERMES BOOKS

John Herington, General Editor

Also available in this series:

HORACE

DAVID ARMSTRONG

Yale University Press
New Haven and London

The translations by James Michie on pp. 88–89 and 91 are reprinted by
permission of the author from *The Odes of Horace* (London: Orion Press, 1963).
All other translations except the author's own are reprinted from *Arion* 9.2–3
(1970) by permission of *Arion* and the following: Burton Raffel and North
Point Press (*Odes* 1.4, pp. 89–90, from Burton Raffel, *The Essential Horace*
[Berkeley, 1983]); and Oxford University Press (*Odes* 2.14, pp. 92–93, from
Basil Bunting, *Collected Poems* [Oxford, 1978]).

Set in Palatino Roman types. Printed in the United States of America by
Vail-Ballou Press, Binghamton, New York.

Library of Congress Cataloging-in-Publication Data

Armstrong, David, 1940–
    Horace / David Armstrong.
        p.   cm. — (Hermes books)
    Bibliography: p.
    Includes index.
    1. Horace—Criticism and interpretation.   I. Title.
    ISBN 0-300-04579-4. — ISBN 0-300-04573-5 (pbk.)
PA6411.A77   1989
874'.01—dc20   89-9045
                                                                   CIP

10   9   8   7   6   5   4   3   2   1

CONTENTS

FOREWORD *by John Herington*   vii

PREFACE   ix

I THE YOUNG HORACE, 65–30 B.C.   1

II HORACE BEFORE AUGUSTUS   26
    The *Satires*
    The *Epodes*

III THE CONQUEST OF A NEW GENRE   68
    Odes 1–3

IV LATER LIFE AND WORKS   117
    Epistles 1 and 2
    Carmen saeculare
    Odes 4

EPILOGUE   163

BIBLIOGRAPHICAL NOTE AND ACKNOWLEDGMENTS   171

INDEX   175

FOREWORD

"IT WOULD BE A PITY," SAID NIETZSCHE, "IF THE CLASSICS SHOULD speak to us less clearly because a million words stood in the way." His forebodings seem now to have been realized. A glance at the increasing girth of successive volumes of the standard journal of classical bibliography, *L'Année philologique*, since World War II is enough to demonstrate the proliferation of writing on the subject in our time. Unfortunately, the vast majority of the studies listed will prove on inspection to be largely concerned with points of detail and composed by and for academic specialists in the field. Few are addressed to the literate but nonspecialist adult or to that equally important person, the intelligent but uninstructed beginning student; and of those few, very few indeed are the work of scholars of the first rank, equipped for their task not merely with raw classical erudition but also with style, taste, and literary judgment.

It is a strange situation. On one side stand the classical masters of Greece and Rome, those models of concision, elegance, and understanding of the human condition, who composed least of all for narrow technologists, most of all for the Common Reader (and, indeed, the Common Hearer). On the other side stands a sort of industrial complex, processing those masters into an annually growing output of technical articles and monographs. What is lacking, it seems, in our society as well as in our scholarship, is the kind of book that was supplied for earlier generations by such men as Richard Jebb and Gilbert Murray in the intervals of their more technical researches—the kind of book that directed the general reader not to the pyramid of secondary literature piled over the burial places of the classical writers but to the living faces of the writers themselves, as perceived by a scholar-humanist with a deep knowledge of, and love for, his subject. Not only for the sake of the potential stu-

dent of classics, but also for the sake of the humanities as a
whole, within and outside academe, it seems that this gap in
classical studies ought to be filled. The Hermes series is a modest attempt to fill it.

We have sought men and women possessed of a rather rare
combination of qualities: a love for literature in other languages,
extending into modern times; a vision that extends beyond academe to contemporary life itself; and above all an ability to express themselves in clear, lively, and graceful English, without
polysyllabic language or parochial jargon. For the aim of the
series requires that they should communicate to nonspecialist
readers, authoritatively and vividly, their personal sense of why
a given classical author's writings have excited people for centuries and why they can continue to do so. Some are classical
scholars by profession, some are not; each has lived long with
the classics, and especially with the author about whom he or
she writes in this series.

The first, middle, and last goal of the Hermes series is to
guide the general reader to a dialogue with the classical masters
rather than to acquaint him or her with the present state of
scholarly research. Thus our volumes contain few or no footnotes; even within the texts, references to secondary literature
are kept to a minimum. At the end of each volume, however, is
a short bibliography that includes recommended English translations and selected literary criticism, as well as historical and
(when appropriate) biographical studies. Throughout, all quotations from the Greek or Latin texts are given in English
translation.

In these ways we hope to let the classics speak again, with a
minimum of modern verbiage (as Nietzsche wished), to the
widest possible audience of interested people.

John Herington

PREFACE

MY INTEREST IN WRITING ABOUT AND TEACHING HORACE'S POETRY
began in the early 1960s, when I was an editor along with
William Arrowsmith and Donald Carne-Ross of what was then a
mildly revolutionary journal of classical literary criticism and
poetic translation, *Arion*. In the end I edited a double issue of
Arion (9.2–3, 1970) devoted entirely to Horace. I still look back
on it with pleasure, for the many various and creative responses
it contained from poets (for example, Robert Fagles's fine Horatian ode on the death of Robert Kennedy) and translators (Paul
Schmidt's version of the breathtaking Latin hexameters on the
theme "Me fabulosae Vulture in Apulo," written as a prize composition by Rimbaud at fourteen; Richard Emil Braun's of the
ode "Otium divos"; and many others) and literary critics classical and modern (including Brooks Otis's "The Relevance of
Horace," still an exemplary introduction, for the reader with no
or little Latin, to what it is like to read some great passages of
Horace in the original, and thirteen delightfully informal pages
of W. K. Wimsatt's on the *Ars poetica*, still not to be found elsewhere). It was astonishingly easy to compile this issue, and it
would not have been easy to evoke a greater variety of responses from living literary people to any other ancient poet,
Homer, Sophocles, and the rest of Horace's betters included. I
have used some of these responses and translations throughout
this book.

It would still be possible to put together such an anthology,
since nearly everyone who has studied a few years of Latin has
some recollection of Horace, but perhaps not quite as easy:
every passing year pushes the classical tradition down a little
further from its position of immemorial privilege in literary education and study. To me that is nothing to be lamented. Such
poetry as Horace's needs no privileged place in education; it

needs just to be presented rightly to win the attention it deserves. In fact, it became clear to me in writing this book that the
scholarship of the last twenty or thirty years has at its best been
engaged in freeing Horace from the dead hand of a misleading
tradition, in which he figured too prominently as an educator of
schoolboys learning Latin grammar and meter from his odes to
be taken seriously as the great poet and complex mind he is. The
death of that tradition has left Horace more free than ever to
make that impression for himself.

Yet one can only say Horace makes an impression "for
himself" while thinking what a paradoxical phrase that is to use
of a poet who was to so great an extent the product of the whole
tradition of Greek and Roman literature before him, and the
generator himself of a long and complex tradition, the "Horatian" tradition, which has lasted from his day to our own in an
endless variety of forms. Horace was an industrious and learned
student of previous literature, and he has been an object of
enthusiasm, love, and intelligent comment to many centuries of
scholars and poets alike. Thus no one can write even the simplest introductory account of him without the most profound
feelings of community with and gratitude to innumerable other
students and lovers of Horace. The design of this series does not
allow elaborate acknowledgments of predecessors in interpretation. I have been able to pay a few of my greatest debts to other
scholars and to friendly readers of my manuscript, by a brief
homage of thanks in the bibliographical note at the end; but if I
were to acknowledge them all, an apparatus of footnotes of little
use to the reader who is not a professional classicist could easily
double the size of this book without adding anything to its message. So intense has been and continues to be the attention
given these few thousand lines of verse by those who understand what is worthwhile in Latin literature.

HORACE

I THE YOUNG HORACE, 65–30 B.C.

EVEN IN OUR WORLD, WHERE NEITHER CLASSICS NOR POETRY HAS as privileged a place in education as they once did, Horace lives on. If his public is smaller now, perhaps both scholars and poets appreciate him more vividly and in better ways than in Victorian and Edwardian times, when Horace survived more as an author read in the original by "every schoolboy" than as a source of inspiration and literary imitation.

The view of Horace that has been gaining ground over the last thirty years seems not so much something new as a revival of older attitudes. For the literary world especially in the period from the early Renaissance to the death of Byron, as for many contemporary writers, Horace was a discovery ever fresh and new. Characteristics that still startle and excite readers who take Horace up unprejudiced made him a hero then. His unique combination of classically "learned," allusive, and perfectly musical Latin verse with apparently free, individualistic self-portraiture, uninhibited by the classical tendency to retreat behind the impersonal poetic voice, piqued readers' curiosity then as it does now. In the old Catholic, royalist Europe, Horace even figured as a liberator. Some of the more liberal-minded and rationalist poets of the Renaissance and the seventeenth century reacted to him with something like ecstasy. They were readers of Horace such as one hopes for nowadays and increasingly finds. Horace excited them: they discovered in him a source of personal integrity in a world bound by monarchical ideology, religious dogma, and the tyranny of family and patronage.

In fact, Horace's peculiar, enduring strength and appeal reside in just this. Though we can at once sympathize with his self-portrait and his poetry, his point of view is independent and personal, and not easily perverted to support the ideology of any age, our own no more than another. The growth of impersonal ideologies as forces in Western culture made many nineteenth-century writers feel guilty about their enjoyment of him, as if it were a retreat from high seriousness into a walled poetic park. But reading Horace is a move into another and deeper seriousness than any merely external account of him can give. To only a superficial reading his style of "autobiographical" poetry yields a picture of a pleasant Roman writer of love and court poetry who enjoys country solitude. Yet terrific confrontations and ironies emerge, and they leave behind a picture more complex and more profound, a model for the individual human mind in its struggle to find and place itself in the confusion of the world.

It is commonplace to say about Horace that the few thousand lines of verse he left behind as his life's work give us a self-portrait of a striking individuality and apparent frankness not easily paralleled in classical literature, certainly not in classical poetry. We can read at vastly greater length what Cicero or the younger Pliny had to say to their friends in correspondence, without getting any such illusion that we know perfectly the person who is speaking, and could (language barriers aside) continue the conversation without difficulty if Horace walked into our presence now.

The feeling of depth and three-dimensionality in this portrait comes from a source we might nowadays find discordant with our first impression of frankness and sincerity. It is built up not just from personal experience, or the words of the Latin language, but from a whole library in Horace's mind of effects, phrases, touches, and contributions to the genres he worked in by poets, dramatists, even prose writers, in Greek and Latin, of every generation from Homer's time to his own.

Here, for example, is what looks like a purely autobiographical memoir of his own freedman father's moral warnings to him in his youth:

> My excellent father gave me the habit
> of avoiding follies by marking down examples:
> when he told me to live modestly, frugally,
> contented with whatever he had to leave me.
> "Don't you see what trouble Albius's son is in,

how Baius is a pauper? That's the true proof:
don't waste your father's fortune." Or when he
    dissuaded me
from some whore's disgraceful charms: "Be unlike
    Scetanius";
or from adultery, when I could have plain, lawful sex:
"Trebonius was caught. Look at his reputation.
Philosophers can give you reasons to shun this
and pursue that. It's enough that I preserve
the ancestral Roman way, and just *tell* you. As long
as you need a guardian, I keep your life
and reputation safe; when time has seasoned
your body and spirit, you can swim without a life-
    jacket."
So he shaped his son with his words: Either he would
    encourage me
to do something—"You have good authority
to do this"—and point to a senator or knight
on the jury lists; or forbid it: "Can you doubt that's
    useless
and dishonorable, when evil gossip consumes
this man, and that man there?"   [*Satires* 1.4.105–26]

No educated listener in Horace's circle can have missed
behind this seemingly autobiographical scene the allusion to *The
Brothers* by the Roman comic playwright Terence, produced
more than a hundred years earlier:

Demea. I keep at it,
I let nothing slide; I train my son; in a word,
I make the boy look into all men's lives as into
a mirror, and take from them examples for himself:
"Do that." *Syrus.* Quite right! *D.* "Avoid that." *S.*
    Truly clever!
D. "That gets you praise." *S.* Just the thing! *D.*
    "That's reprehensible."
S. Excellent! *D.* And moreover . . . . *S.* Oh goodness,
    I haven't time
for any more just now . . . .   [*Adelphoe* 413–20]

Horace's father is drawn from literature as much as from life. This would have surprised no educated Roman reader: Terence himself was borrowing from the Greek comic writer Menander, who in turn was probably taking a hint from Plato. But it is not the sort of thing modern readers expect at all (unless perhaps from writers like Joyce). We tend to differentiate between consciously allusive literary art and "sincerity." Is Horace remembering his father talking or Terence's Demea? To ask this question is not necessarily to cast doubt on Horace's personal sincerity. Readers from Ariosto to Byron appreciated perfectly that this unobtrusive hiding of intellectual riches makes the impression of personality one gets from reading Horace deeper, not shallower. What *sort* of allusion a writer picks is itself a declaration of personality. By making the reader bring all he can to his understanding of a verse, the poet conveys a sense of the depth and layers that human personalities possess in real life. This technique is gradually being lost to the modern world. It is a fitting tribute to Horace's cleverness and artistry that passages by his imitators—such writers as Ariosto, Montaigne, Marvell, Pope, Voltaire, and Byron—are often most sincerely self-revelatory when most indebted to Horace himself. Without his memory of literature to help create it, there would be no portrait of Horace. In the same way, all of those writers' personalities would appear to us somewhat different, some of them very different, if Horace had not written.

It must be admitted that Horace is as elusive as he is allusive, but in the end, part of what he says about himself must be as true of the real person as of his carefully constructed poetic self-presentation. Literal-minded critics of an earlier generation tend to annoy the modern reader by taking every statement Horace makes about himself in the poems as fact (except when they want to reduce his sex life to more decorous proportions by evaporating his lovers into poetic fictions). But there is another extreme to avoid. What little we know about Horace from sources other than himself seems to suggest that his elaborate self-portrait is not all fiction by any means. A biographer can probably credit what Horace says about his education, his property, his position, and his social circle and their ways. Whether his father "really" talked like Demea is another question. It will easily be seen from what follows what sort of thing in the poems I take to be accurate information about the "historical" Horace.

It seems astonishing today to think of Horace, a freedman's son who, aside from his literary life, was mainly remarkable for being one of the most successful arrivistes in Roman social history, as a liberating influence in the history of thought. But he was once, and deserved to be, a favorite refuge of the independent and freethinking spirits of Europe from the Renaissance to the end of the Enlightenment. In some ways Horace was much dearer to them than the more radically agnostic and skeptical poet Lucretius, with whom for centuries he tended to be paired by freethinkers, especially in France and England. He was so much less alienated and alienating than Lucretius, and thus provided a more reassuring psychological model for living and surviving in a world whose religious and social assumptions contradicted commonsense.

Horace can still refresh, still liberate even in the modern world, if we encounter him (as we mostly do now) simply as one poet among many instead of a canonized "classic." Indeed, he may well be one of the few ancient writers to benefit substantially from the withering of the great European tradition of literature and literary scholarship. The joys of reading and discovering Horace are still there for every modern reader to find on his own. But he has to be very careful what explanatory reading he chooses, at least among books published since about the 1820s, when literature began its long, unhappy progress out of the hands of poets and creators in every genre and into the hands of academics.

The necrotic influence of the conventional Victorian attitude toward Horace still exists, though it is fortunately fading. In decades past, academic botanists of European literature conscientiously memorized epithets to tag a "Horatian" satire (as opposed to a "Juvenalian" one) or a "Horatian" love lyric (as opposed to one more in the style of Sappho or Catullus), when perpetrated by Boileau or Malherbes, by Pope or Marvell. Thus Horatian satire is quiet, personal, and reflective; Juvenalian satire is obscene, unsparing, uncompromising. Horatian love lyrics preach disengagement, resignation, moderation, and good-humor; Sappho and Catullus are all unreflective and romantic passion, counting no cost.* Such definitions are as gross a misrepresentation of Juvenal, Catullus, and Sappho as of Horace, but they still hurt. After all, if the best the advertisement can do is "quiet, reflective, moderate," even an academic can be forgiven for turning instead to the book billed as "shocking, passionate, uncompromising" by his potted history of Latin literature. Insofar as the word *Horatian* survives in modern usage, it suggests indifference, lack of commitment, and a world of private pleasures. I have been told by more than one American poet that *Horatian* is now used mainly in castigating other poets for being too purely esthetic to care about radical politics.

Brigid Brophy was the most engaging of the "negative" responders to my questionnaire in the *Arion* issue about what Horace meant to the literary world of today. She said humorously that as a schoolgirl she had been fascinated by the phrase in *Odes* 1.38 where the poet is making a garland to wear while drinking, *mitte sectari, rosa quo locorum / sera moretur*, which she had translated to herself as "Send to inquire, in what place the rose lingers late." But at Oxford she discovered to her confusion that *mitte* is short for *omitte*, "do not inquire." That seemed typical, she complained: every time Horace conjures up some "baroque extravagant gesture," as a poet should, he seems to back off and advise against it.

In reality, and in the context of his whole work, that seems characteristic only of the anthology pieces deliberately chosen by teachers in the days when Horace was still a school-poet. There is no lack of baroque extravagant gestures in his poetry, and there are scenes of terrific sensuality. Take the ode "Quantum distet ab Inacho" (3.19), in which Horace says the exact opposite, that he will have nothing to do with hands that are sparing of roses:

---

*The distinction between "Horatian" and "Juvenalian" satire is of course Dryden's (*Discourse Concerning the Original and Progress of Satire*, 1693), but the first full demonstration of how pernicious and useless it is to criticism is apparently Niall Rudd's "Dryden on Horace and Juvenal" (appendix to his *Satires of Horace* [Cambridge, 1966]).

How many generations separate Inachus
from Codrus, who faced death for his fatherland,
and the genealogy of Aeacus—this you relate to us,
and the wars of dreadful Troy;
as for how much a cask of Chian wine costs
and who's to heat and mix in the water,
whose house is offered us, how quickly
I can shut out this winter, not a word.
Slave, pour a drink for the new moon,
for midnight—hurry!—then for the augurship
of Murena: three parts wine to one of water,
or make it nine, the Muses' number:
I love them: triple winecups tripled
are the poet's lightning; three to one
the Graces ordain, fearing brawls,
dancing in simple nakedness;
but I'd rather run wild. Why are the flutes quiet,
why is the lyre with them on the wall?
I hate a thrifty hand: scatter roses.
Let jealous Lycus hear the crazy din
and the girl next door, ill-married to his age:
Young Rhode—Rosy—adores you, Telephus, young
as Hesperus, and your thick bright hair;
a slower flame for Glycera warms me.

"I hate a thrifty hand: scatter roses." A poem like this has
nothing sober about it but the structure: "the hard shell of his
verses, a pattern of Latin thrift," as Lawrence Durrell put it. We
learn in the first four verses that Telephus is a poet and a learned
one, in the last that he is young and beautiful. Death, that fre-
quent guest at Horatian feasts, is delicately hinted at in the fate
of Codrus and the mention of Troy. The middle is taken up with
Horace's instructions for a drunken poets' party, with the strong
wine drunk nearly straight, one part water to nine of wine. The
noise is to disturb the ill-matched pair next door; the party may
be in honor of Maecenas's brother-in-law, Varro Murena, newly
appointed augur (and destined to die miserably in a conspiracy
against Augustus shortly after the *Odes* were published in 23
B.C.). But the patron is only the pretext, and we are left happily

uncertain as to whether he is there (probably not), or whether
anyone is there but the well-matched older and younger pair of
lovers, and what is to happen later.

A teasing, difficult poem, more for poets than professors,
who get impatient with blanks in the scenario that admit of
filling in several ways rather than one "right" way. Horace intentionally mocks all his readers but the original addressee by
never telling them, any more than Telephus did, how much the
wine cost, whose house this is, and so on. But it shows that
Horace is not well characterized by the simpler poems many
people remember. He has been saddled increasingly, since his
vogue in the eighteenth century and the Age of Reason, with
the image of a poet of reason. In that picture, Horace is a poet of
middle age and golden mediocrity, a freedman's son who, after
briefly daring all with Brutus at Philippi, sank into the life of a
government clerk, singing love affairs of just the right casual
level of involvement, the praises of the emperor and patron who
paid him, and both in lyric and satire the "kind placidity" of the
reasonable man, or rather, the good-natured selfish man.

But Horace's poetry is actually full, consciously filled, with
the tension between restraint and excess, and it is not a tension
between poetry and a prosy mind. On the one hand are the
poignant images of Horace's real experience, and all-but-fatal
fascination, with every sort of extravagance of emotion, of sexuality and luxury and greed and grief and the terror of death: the
feelings of a rich and relatively secure man in a dangerous society where the privileged lived extravagantly and lacked nothing
but time. On the other hand is ancient morality, that hard, wary
attitude to life and experience, expressed in maxim after prover-
bial maxim, which all the great Greek and Roman poets shared
with the humblest farmers and slaves in their audience. Even
the most elegant, learned, and cynical peppered their verses
with maxims in the same spirit as Horace did. *Carpe diem, quam
minimum credula postero*, the most famous of all his tags—"Pluck
the day, believe as little as possible in the next"—is as much in
that vein as any.

On the other hand, too, is a harsh Roman survivor men-
tality made all the more vivid by Horace's own experience of life:

a boyhood spent in Rome as Pompey and Caesar tore the Republic apart; his expensive philosophical studies in Athens, abruptly ended for two years' service as a high officer in Brutus's ill-starred army, with Philippi and the confiscation of his lands as a reward; and in his later years under Augustus, enough previsions of the coming evils of absolutism, of the *cruenta domus Caesarum*, the "bloody house of Caesars," to cause him to worry about whether he was doing well to be Augustus's laureate. All that emerges clearly enough from any consideration of his life and work in the context of his times. Modern readers may not immediately perceive this tension between Horace's rise to wealth and security and the violent stresses of his political environment. But readers in the sixteenth and seventeenth centuries saw this tension first and foremost, and it made Horace a sympathetic figure to them. It was this side of Horace that appealed to Ariosto and to Sir Thomas Wyatt, for example, as they wrote their "Horatian" satires at the courts of the Este and of Henry VIII; or to Andrew Marvell in the world of the English Civil War and the Restoration, adapting Horace's tense, reserved praises of Augustus, a new ruler who could still fail, to Oliver Cromwell. Modern historical scholarship has done much to help us see Horace's life in a light that makes their sympathy and enthusiasm understandable.

In 91 B.C. there was a general uprising among Rome's Italian subjects, the *socii* or "allies." Since the Punic Wars those in the South had served as a buffer between Rome and the Greeks of southern Italy and Sicily; they had been exploited as suppliers of manpower for the Roman legions without being given the rights of Roman citizens in recompense. Among the cities that joined this uprising, the Social or Marsic War, was Venusia, a two-hundred-year-old Latin colony in the rural inland part of Apulia. Its citizens had the inferior form of Roman citizenship called "Latin rights," *ius Latii*, and were not at all content with it. The first campaigns went badly for the Romans. Their empire was threatened abroad, they needed the Italians' loyalty and manpower, and they were compelled to offer the full Roman franchise to all Italy before they could win. Venusia suffered badly. It was taken in 88, a year before the war ended, and three thousand of its freemen sold into slavery. But its citizens at last became Romans.

Enrolled among these new citizens, before long, was Horace's father. The elder Horace was a freed slave, perhaps one of the poor citizens enslaved in 88; at any rate, he was evidently a native Italian, like many slaves of this period in Italy, whether born to slavery or not. Horace never speaks of himself as anything other than Italian by birth. The Social War, and the great slave rebellion of Spartacus that raged through southern Italy in 73–71, are dim traditions to Horace, who was born after they were over. They were great events in his father's life: because Venusia was now Roman, his own status as a freedman was entirely changed.

Roman slaves employed at hard labor almost certainly would live and die slaves. But those talented slaves who called themselves to their masters' notice by being useful in business, amusing, or attractive could often succeed in getting themselves manumitted after as little as five or six years' adult service, when they were between twenty-five and thirty. They would pay from their savings, to which they had a legal right, the 5 percent tax on their market value that the state exacted for manumissions, often in addition promising their former master various free services by contract. In the city many poorer citizens even paid the tax themselves and freed their few slaves to put them, as new Roman citizens, on the grain dole and save the cost of food. In the last century B.C. the *vicesima libertatis* was one of the major sources of the treasury's revenue. Once freed, Roman citizens' slaves became full citizens. They wore the toga and (if they lived in Rome or were ready to travel there) voted in elections. Only the freeborn (including freedmen's sons), however, could hold the next higher rank in Roman society, that of *eques* ("knight"). Even freedmen who could prove the large property qualification this rank required were debarred from it by custom, though not by law. Custom, not law, also effectively disqualified freedmen's sons (though not their grandsons) from the highest rank, that of senator.

The system thus gave successful freedmen and their families a powerful motivation to increase their fortune and position over several generations until their slave origin could be forgotten, and they could be members of the governing classes on more or less equal terms. Horace's father, who had a talent for business, obviously worked very hard at it with just this motivation. Indeed, the Roman upper classes' snobbery about freedmen and their sons was almost explicitly a kind of business-oriented motivational trick to encourage, not discourage, their ambition. Senators were theoretically debarred from business dealings and required to live on the income of their land. In practice, they dealt largely in trade and commerce through freedmen agents. Roman economic life depended on the ambition of freedmen and their families to become respectable to such an extent that the barriers could be let down only so far. On the other hand, the peace of society depended on their feeling real hopes of advancement to such an extent that the barriers could be raised only so high and no further.

Horace's father at first belonged somewhere in the middle of this class. When he gained his freedom, he took what was a common route to financial independence in a poorly monetized age: he went into business as a *coactor*, or collector of goods for auction. These men converted revenues in kind—anything from farm and household goods to expensive real estate—into coin for private businessmen, or the Roman state, or both; and the more prosperous ones were more like bankers than auctioneers. Many freedmen and their sons and many free Romans made a good living in this profession. It was looked on with calculated contempt by the senatorial and equestrian aristocracy, a prejudice Horace modestly pretends to share. But many *coactores* and *praecones* (auctioneers) managed to raise their sons to equestrian rank. L. Aelius, a contemporary whose father was a praeco, became a distinguished teacher and scholar and an eques, but had to endure the significant nicknames Stilo ("scribbler") and Praeconinus ("auctioneer's boy") from his better-born friends. Horace's father, like L. Aelius Stilo Praeconinus's, seems to have made at least an equestrian or senatorial fortune (four hundred thousand sesterces of ratable property, which translates into about one thousand modern troy ounces of gold, currently worth about four hundred thousand dollars), and probably two or three times that, in this "humble" calling. Not long after

Horace's birth at Venusia on December 8, 65 B.C., he was able to move with his son to Rome, already by far the most expensive city in the ancient world.

There he set out to push his child—whom he must soon have perceived to be brilliant—as high in Roman society as he could be made to go, by educating Horace expensively with the sons of the senatorial aristocracy and supervising that education himself. Literature opened to the clever every kind of advancement, both in the government's lucrative service and in society, if the aristocracy found them amusing; and the young Horace proved to be a spectacular success in both ways.

In two famous passages Horace describes his life in Rome with his father. In the first, already quoted, his father appears as a practical teacher, though a little insecure before the fine things Horace's literary and philosophical teachers supposedly know. In the other, Horace looks back with gratitude on his father's decision not to waste him on a humble trade school in Venusia, but to send him to such fashionable Roman literary teachers as Orbilius of Beneventum, a crabby enthusiast of the now-antiquated Latin poetry of the third and second centuries B.C.:

> If my nature is to have few and middling faults,
> honest otherwise, as if on a handsome physique
> you could find some scattered warts to reprehend;
> if no one can reproach me with greed or meanness
> or a taste for filthy nightlife; if I live in purity
> (to sing my own praise) and innocence, dear to my
>   friends,
> my father was the cause. Low-born, and not rich in
>   land,
> he would not have me sent to Flavius's day school,
> where hulking centurions' hulking louts of sons,
> with pack and tablets hung on their left arms,
> went clutching their eight brass pennies on the ides;
> but dared to take his son to Rome and teach him
> whatever studies the greatest knight or senator
> would teach his sons.   [*Satires* 1.6.65–78]

No doubt Horace's father was sincere in assuring him that it was all right if in the end Horace rose no higher than himself.

But the aspirations of a wealthy freedman for a talented son, in the later days of the Republic, could be high indeed. Equestrian rank could be Horace's with enough money and the right military service behind him. This was not common for a freedman's son, but not unknown either. The money was there; the rank could be attained with the right patrons. Even more daringly, freedmen's sons were taking advantage of the confusion of Roman society to skip a generation and push themselves into the lower ranks of the Senate. This was not difficult, in a city so crowded with freedmen as Rome. Election to the lowest magistracy, the quaestorship, made one eligible for membership in the Senate for life; and senators of that low rank could avoid notice, never speak in meetings, and still enjoy enormous legal and social privileges. The richest and best-born of the new Roman citizens from Italy could afford to dispense with these privileges. People of Horace's standing felt differently.

The citizens' rolls and those of the Senate and the equestrian orders were reviewed and revised every five years. This was called a *census*, and the officials who took it, the *censores*, usually tried to expel freedmen's sons from the Senate. But the turbulence of the last decades of the Republic and the enormous influx of new citizens made the census increasingly difficult to take. The last complete review before Augustus was in 70 B.C., when the censors discovered a freedman's son in the ranks and duly expelled him, but allowed him to continue wearing the senator's toga in recognition that he had held office legally. In 50, when Horace was fifteen, a conservative censor who favored the party of Pompey and the Senate expelled all freedmen's sons—now more numerous—from the Senate, but the gesture was so unpopular that it helped Julius Caesar's cause, not Pompey's. Not much more than a year later, the party of Pompey and the Senate went down before Caesar at Pharsalia. In recruiting the Senate's decimated ranks, which he raised from six hundred to nearly nine hundred, the new dictator, whose support depended on the army, the municipal Italians, and the business classes, pointedly included select freedmen's sons, along with centurions from the army and magnates from all over Italy and even Cisalpine Gaul.

So it is probably no coincidence that, in 46 or 45 B.C.,

Horace's father decided to send him to study philosophy at Athens on equal terms with the sons of the greatest Roman nobility. It must have cost a great deal. Cicero's son, who later served, like Horace, under Brutus, went to Athens at the same time on eighty thousand sesterces a year, the net income of about one million sesterces in urban rental property which his father assigned him for the purpose. Cicero, hopefully writing to Atticus in Greece, asks him to hold up to his son two other young noblemen (who became Horace's fellow officers in Brutus's army and remained lifelong friends) as examples of students who can live comfortably on the same allowance (*Letters to Atticus* 12.32). The younger Cicero overspent his allowance anyway; about the other two we do not know.

Horace says little about his years in Athens; only that he wrote Greek verses there, before he decided on Latin as his medium (*Satires* 1.10.31ff.), and that he learned "to seek truth in the grove of Academe," *inter silvas Academi quaerere verum* (*Epistles* 2.2.45). The common lessons of Greek philosophy, especially ethical philosophy, were a standard element of upper-class education and of well-bred Roman talk, and play a large part in Horace's poetry. He seems to have learned them as well as any Roman, that is to say, in broad outline rather than in what well-bred Roman students thought niggling detail. In particular, he shares the common Roman tendency to overemphasize the ethical side of the various philosophies he learned, which was felt to be a better guide for the serious man's life-style, and more useful for literary application in rhetoric or poetry, than metaphysics or logic. That does not mean Horace was a smatterer in this or any other field of literature; his poems show that he was a hard and diligent reader all his life.

He also made himself a large circle of aristocratic and noble *amici*, which means "patrons" or "allies" in politics and art as much as "friends": in upper-class Roman life the notions were not separable. He learned at Athens to share their political opinions, if indeed he had not before; Horace's father sounds like an admirer of the established order. "There are even freedmen who are Optimates," Cicero had said in his review of the various social classes that composed the Senate's party (*Pro Sestio* 97). The kind of concern Horace claims his father taught him for the conservative moral and social prejudices of the Roman electorate suggests that the elder Horace was himself an example. And few ancient businessmen bothered with theoretical criticism of a system under which they had themselves prospered.

The city of Athens in this period tended to exercise its nominal liberty as a free city of the Roman Empire on the side of the Optimates in Roman politics, no doubt influenced by the heavy spending of visiting Roman senators and their student sons. Athens had recently been punished, although not severely, for supporting Pompey and the Senate against Julius Caesar, who indulgently accepted Athens's surrender after his victory at Pharsalia, saying he would allow the city to be saved by its illustrious dead. Caesar was assassinated in March 44 B.C. In February of the next year the liberator and tyrannicide Marcus Brutus arrived in Athens, discouraged by his failure to build an effective following for his cause either in Rome or Italy, and still uncertain of his future plans. He was joined shortly after by Cassius. Their reception by the Athenians and the young Roman nobles studying in Athens changed everything. They found themselves received as legendary heroes. The Athenians erected their statues by the side of the ancient statues of Harmodius and Aristogeiton, whose act of tyrannicide ended the rule of the Peisistratids in the sixth century B.C. and cleared the way for Athens's first real democracy. Brutus was at last in a position to raise legions and take over Greece and Macedonia, while Cassius secured Syria and the East. Together they prepared to face the joint heirs of Caesar's dictatorship, Antony and Octavian.

Horace was offered, and accepted, an appointment in the liberators' army as *tribunus militum* (one of the six junior officers directly responsible to the legate who commanded a legion). "Tribune of the soldiers," the usual post for young men who intended to enter the Senate, automatically conferred equestrian rank on the holders. This military rank was uncommon for freedmen's sons, and Horace pictured himself later in life as still remembering with indignation the taunts of his fellow officers and the soldiers (*Satires* 1.6.45–48).

One can only imagine how Horace's father would have rejoiced in this appointment, if he had lived to hear of it. He seems, however, to have died while Horace was in Athens, and probably before Brutus's war began. His rejoicing, however, might have been tempered somewhat by his son's danger, which was real. If he intended Horace to succeed among the *nobiles*, he probably also intended him to avoid at all costs the intense danger in which the upper classes of this period lived. The Social War had been played out against a background of savage massacres and proscriptions among the great men of the Republic and their supporters: the struggles of Marius and Sulla. The age of Caesar and Pompey had seen yet more; the nobiles were decimated again in the great battles between Caesar and the Pompeians at Pharsalia, Thapsus, and Munda. Horace was risking his life to help take Macedonia from Antony's brother, its legal governor, then helping Brutus and Cassius brutally pillage the rich cities of Asia Minor for money. (Brutus and Cassius embodied the worst features of the old Republic in their belief that provincials' property existed mainly to further their own ambitions.) Meanwhile, in Italy, Antony and Octavian were executing, and confiscating the property of, senators by the dozens and knights by the hundreds. Horace's father would surely have wished his son to stay quietly on the sidelines whoever won, but instead Horace followed along through the grim business of plundering provincials to finance the war, and then went on with the liberators to Philippi. There they died, and many of Horace's friends with them, Brutus quoting a lost Greek tragedy:

> O wretched Virtue, so you were a word;
> I worshipped you as if you were a fact;
> yet all along you were the slave of Fortune.

Philippi was no minor disaster for Rome. According to Horace's friend and patron Messalla, who wrote memoirs of the period, some twenty-five thousand soldiers were killed on the first day of the battle alone (Plutarch *Brutus* 45.1). Horace later remembered the contrast between the carefree wine parties in Athens (or on the march?) and the shock of combat in a poem he wrote, under Augustus's regime, to a fellow officer in Brutus's army who had finally returned to Italy after serving (probably)

with Antony in Egypt. Probably, for Pompeius seems to have
needed Horace's help ("beneath my laurel") to win pardon from
Augustus, who may even be "Jove" here:

> You who faced man's ultimate hour with me
> so often when Brutus led our soldiering,
> who has given you back, a citizen,
> to Roman gods and Italian sky,
> Pompeius, first of my boon companions?
> I broke up the lingering day with you so often,
> crowning our shining hair
> with garlands and with Syrian nard.
> I felt with you Philippi, the headlong rout,
> the small shield left* disgracefully, virtue broken,
> those who had been courageous talkers
> sprawled chin-first on the filthy ground.
> But winged Mercury took me above the hosts,
> lifted me, shuddering, through the dark air;
> the sea-tides pulled you back again
> into the wars through boiling surf.
> Then pay to Jove the feast you owe him,
> protect your side that aches with war
> beneath my laurel; show no mercy
> to the winecasks I marked for you.
> Spill the great shells of perfumed oil,
> keep filling this Egyptian winecup
> till you forget. Someone tear myrtle
> branches and twist them with water-parsley
> for garlands; someone ask the dice
> who's master of revels.† I will drink harder

*Whether Horace abandoned his *own* shield, the ultimate disgrace, is left
ambiguous in the Latin, unless the reminiscence of the archaic Greek poet Archilochus (who cheerfully threw away his own to save his life) is meant to hint that
Horace means he did so too.

†Literally: "Who will hurry up crowns from myrtle and water-parsley?
Whom will Venus [the name of the high throw in Roman dice-playing] name
master of drinking?"—for Roman drinking parties chose an arbiter to decree
how strong the wine should be mixed and how it should be served. A little
above, Pompeius is supposed to fill his ciborium or Egyptian-style winecup with

than all the Bacchae. It's pure pleasure
to go crazy. My friend is saved.   [*Odes* 2.7]

After Philippi, Horace's own dangers were over. The victors, Octavian and Antony, were more interested in building up their respective factions in the state than in vengeance, and such of his aristocratic friends as survived—Valerius Messalla and Calpurnius Bibulus, for example—were immediately forgiven and welcomed into Antony's entourage. Horace returned to Italy to find that his lands, like the rest of those around Venusia, had been confiscated for distribution to Octavian's soldiers. But he still had the money and influence to buy himself a brilliant government job, that of *scriba quaestorius* or clerk to the young senators, the quaestors, who were in charge of the public treasury, the *aerarium*. One bought the tenure and salary of this position for life, and Horace appears to have kept it till he died.

The scribes were the highest in rank of the permanent staff of the annually changing senatorial magistrates, the *apparitores*, whose ranks included freedmen and their sons, but also many equestrians and many literary and learned men whose patrons had advanced them to these comfortable jobs as a reward for talent. They had a good salary and the far more important opportunity of earning commissions for collecting and registering the state revenues. Since the aerarium was also a state archive, they were paid extra for making authentic copies of government documents and decrees. The commissions were so lucrative that they were rotated, and a scribe was only allowed to serve in Rome one year out of three. He could collect fat fees, however, in off-years for managing government finances in the provinces—something Horace, who traveled little outside Italy for the rest of his life, did not bother with.

As it was, Horace soon restored his fortunes. By the time of his first publication, the first book of *Satires*, in 35 B.C., he was rich enough to stand for quaestor and become a senator (at

---

"forgetful Massic," a Campanian wine. In the next line, Horace says he will drink "more insanely than the Edonians" or Thracians, famous for their orgies in honor of Dionysus. Where I have paraphrased or changed the syntax in translating, I hope my liberties usually go little further than this.

thirty he was just becoming eligible), though he explains at some length, in his sixth satire, that he was by then too indifferent to rank to put up with the ridicule other freedmen's sons incurred by doing so. He had been ridiculed and abused for being a military tribune with such parentage, he says, and that was enough. He represents himself, in a brilliant joke, as an equestrian happy to be allowed to ride a mule (not the regulation horse) by himself on his travels from Rome "as far as Tarentum," rather than making himself ridiculous with the show of slaves and grooms that were expected to attend senators in public (*Satires* 1.6.104–11). He was able, also, to own a house in Rome with numerous slaves and a stable—no small achievement in a city that had been so expensive for many generations that even visiting kings sometimes rented third-floor walkups.

It took Octavian and Antony a decade (41–31) to come to the final resolution of their differences at Actium, just as it had taken the earlier triumvirs, Caesar and Pompey, a decade (59–49) to come to their final contest at Pharsalia. Octavian and Antony had preempted, as triumvirs, the right of nomination to the higher offices and thus to the higher reaches of the Senate, but the lower ones were competed for with liveliness by anyone who could afford to, including scribes, freedmen's sons, and even rich freedmen themselves. At Rome the forms of life in a free city and much of the reality persisted with little change. The law courts, to which Horace belonged as an equestrian juror, were full of loud and lively financial quarrels. If the old free Republic died completely, as some claim, with the proscriptions in 43 or at Philippi in 42, one would not discover that from the writings of the young Horace. The dinner parties of the new rich of the era, full of showy, indigestible novelties, supplied spectacular opportunities for his satiric verse, though working out the details of this long-vanished cuisine is a little fatiguing to a modern reader.

What is not at all fatiguing is to follow Horace's pictures of the other tasteless excesses of an age of anxiety. These were Horace's formative years as a writer, and we can study his life and attitudes in this period, from age twenty-four to thirty-four, in the two books of *Satires* (35 and 30 B.C.) and the book of *Epodes* (published in 29 B.C., although some probably were written much earlier). They offer an interesting picture of Horace, or would if his critics of the last hundred years had done anything much to bring it out as a whole. This Horace was much more of a ruthless and self-seeking social climber than a young "Roman Socrates," as optimists have sometimes called him. He also bears a great deal more resemblance to an interesting human being, and to understand him this way makes some of the traits most complained of in the mature Horace not only forgivable but touching, inevitable, and endearing. If the *Odes* and *Epistles* had been lost, Horace would still figure as one of the greatest of Roman poets just because of these three books of youthful poems. They are less elevated than his later poems in subject and even language (for they deal in the untrammeled Latin of the people and the older Latin poets much more freely than the later poems). They are sometimes grandiose and political, and sometimes light and elegant, but they are also full of unsparing pictures of Roman low-life, and they work in the amoral humor of the Roman vulgar—of popular street songs and graffiti—to great effect.

With a raw, youthful, physical energy that the poems superficially disclaim, Horace portrays himself as devoting his many leisure hours in the 30s to literature, to winning himself a still higher place in society than he already had, to dinner parties, and to sexual pleasure. He first won the friendship of the poet Vergil, who had early attached himself to Octavian's following, and then the friendship which dictated the shape of his whole future life— that of Vergil's extraordinary patron, Maecenas, to whom Vergil and his circle introduced Horace in 39 or 38. It is noteworthy that from the first, and throughout the thirties B.C., Vergil was Octavian's poet far more than Maecenas's; with Horace, the reverse was true. To the young Horace, Octavian is something more, but not much more, than an important Roman politician, a friend of a friend. Indeed, it was only much later in Horace's life, in the fourth book of odes (13 B.C.), that he gave in to imperial pressure and acknowledged him, now the Emperor Augustus, as chief patron of his verses.

Horace's relation to Maecenas was different. Gaius Maecenas, five or ten tears older than Horace, was an Etruscan from Arretium (modern Arezzo), and ostentatiously traced his descent on both sides from the ancient princes, *lucumones*, of Etruscan cities. The Etruscan nobility cared little for the Roman virtues of devotion to business, politics, and patriotism, and Maecenas was the first and last Etruscan since the expulsion of the last of the ancient kings of Rome, the Etruscan Tarquins, to become a central figure in Roman political history. He was both the greatest of Horace's many powerful amici and his intimate, lifelong friend. He had been a trusted counselor of Octavian since Caesar's death brought them both to Rome in 44, and was at the head of all his affairs in Rome and Italy, but chose to remain equestrian in rank, refusing to associate himself with the Senate or to behave in public like a Roman official. He was famous for conducting public and private business *discinctus*, with his tunic left loose, flowing, and unbelted. Because that is also the Latin word for "loose," "fast," or "lazy," it brought Maecenas much satirical criticism, which he ignored. Neither did he care if people satirized his many love affairs, which like Horace's (assuming Horace tells the truth about himself in this point, as is probable) were bisexual, but showed a preference for women; or his stormy relationship, unfaithful on both sides, with his capricious and beautiful young wife Terentia.

Maecenas was immensely rich, and by the time of the first book of satires he was tearing down half the Esquiline hill to build his famous Roman palace and gardens. He was devoted to gourmandise, and the elder Pliny seems thankful that such fashionable contributions to Rome's cuisine as young donkey's flesh did not outlast Maecenas. Whatever his reputation with the more old-fashioned nobles, Maecenas was immensely popular with the Roman people, and his reputation for good nature was so great that even Seneca, in the middle of a long satirical disquisition on his character and writings (*Letters to Lucilius* 114.7), pauses to say that "his great glory was his mildness; he spared the sword and abstained from blood, nor did he make a show of his power in anything but his license of manners; but even this praise he spoiled by his monstrous affectations as a writer, which make clear that he was not gentle, merely soft."

Maecenas was in fact a Roman author of at least the low second rank, since Seneca and Quintilian, among others, read him and took him seriously enough to criticize him. He wrote a

Symposium (which we would love to have) in which he, Vergil, Horace, and Valerius Messalla were the chief interlocutors. He wrote short poems, and a great deal of ambitiously artificial prose, whose chief fault seems to have been that it used techniques only appropriate to poetry, and rather high poetry at that. The one short poem that survives complete is famous for its paraphrasable content rather than its beauty:

> Paralyze my hands, my feet and ankles,
> put a swollen hunch on my back,
> shake the last of my teeth loose:
> as long as life lasts, it is well: even stuck
> to a sharp cross, keep me living!

Seneca, who quotes this poem (*Letters to Lucilius* 101.10), criticizes it as cowardly and a revelation of Maecenas's effeminacy. Most readers have felt its existential *horror mortis* rather as a relief from the conventional Roman stoicism about death, but the least of Horace's own many reflections on death are worth ten of it even in that light.

Typical of the many deeply affectionate references to Maecenas in Horace's early poems is a passage from *Satires* 2.6, published in 30 B.C. and thanking Maecenas for the gift of the Sabine farm. Horace contrasts what is by now his crowded business life in Rome with his peaceful life among his tenant farmers. But his pretended distaste for the crowd and business is a mere screen for his pleasure in showing off his intimacy with Maecenas and the influence and respect it has gotten him:

> But the moment I've come to the shadowy Esquiline
> dozens of other men's business leaps for my head
> and sides. "Tomorrow at seven, Roscius
> begged you to appear for his case at the praetor's
> court."
> "Quintus, the scribes are meeting today on important
> new business that's come up; you said you'd attend;
> they begged you." "Please see that Maecenas's signet
> is impressed on these tablets." "I'll try." "You can if
> you want!"
> he retorts, and won't leave. Nearer eight years than
> seven

> since Maecenas began to consider me one of his own,
> but just as the sort of man to take in his carriage
> when he travels, and trust with trivial conversation:
> "What time is it?" "Can the Thracian Rooster take on
> Syrus?"* "This morning chill can bite a man
> if he's not careful"—such things as are well confided
> to leaky ears. All these years, hour by hour,
> your poet's more subject to envy: "He" has watched
>   the games
> with me! We have exercised in the Campus Martius!
> "Son of Fortune," everyone calls me. A frightening
>   rumor
> runs from the Rostrum down to the city alleys.
> Whoever I see consults me: "Dear fellow, for you
> must know, you live with the gods: what of the
>   Dacians?"
> "I've heard nothing." "You're always the ironist,
>   aren't you?" "Nothing;
> may the gods pursue me with vengeance if I lie."
>
> [*Satires* 2.6.24–55]

Later poems only reinforce the impression. In Horace's lyric poems to Maecenas one finds intentional traces of the language other Latin poets use for intense romantic relationships—of Catullus's to Lesbia or Propertius's to Cynthia. One also finds what there is in him, besides the description of a father already dead when he began writing, of the language of familial affection. Horace never married, and even makes a joke of it to Maecenas in one of the odes:

> You're wondering what a bachelor would do
> on the calends of March; what can they mean here,
> flowers and incense-caskets, and live coals
>   in the fresh-cut turf;
> you know all the lore of Greece and Rome . . . .
>
> [*Odes* 3.8.1–5]

All the lore, the poet goes on, except the private ritual Horace has invented. The first of March is the Matronalia, the day of

*Two gladiators.

presents from husbands to wives and other family rituals, but also the day Horace was nearly killed by a falling tree. That day he celebrates annually, in fulfillment of a vow. He invites Maecenas, who has dropped in, to spend the evening, indeed the whole night, drinking together with him to his salvation, and to forget the city's affairs and troubles—a Matronalia for stags.

No doubt Horace was a more pleasant person than Stendhal's Julien Sorel, the ambitious young peasant whose love affairs take him tragically high in aristocratic society in *The Red and the Black*; but he had something of Sorel's psychological makeup and his cold ambition, and he paid a price for it, both personally and artistically. All of us who read Horace find different ways to put it, but they amount to the same thing: his survival and his success cost him something emotionally. If his poems are an index of his personality, even in general outline, Horace was always attractive and attracted to women, like Stendhal's heroes, but he never attached himself to one woman romantically and passionately. In this he perhaps resembled the typical Roman of his day more than the great love poets like Catullus or Propertius. What is more surprising, he never married or had children, though that is the one feature of his career that genuinely would have pained the old freedman who so enthusiastically helped his only son get ahead in school at Rome and Athens. There would be no wife, and no grandson, to inherit the house at Rome, the Sabine farm, and the rest of the considerable wealth and influence Horace had acquired by the time he died, or to carry on the name the old freedman had been so anxious to found.

Horace tends to avoid the subject of family life. His many odes and epistles to friends contain surprisingly few references to their wives and children, and those few are for the most part very distant. Even Augustus's wife Livia and his sister Octavia are mentioned only once each, in *Odes* 3.14—*unico gaudens mulier marito . . . soror clari ducis*, "his wife, rejoicing in such an outstanding husband . . . our great leader's sister," neither among Horace's more jeweled phrases. There are no condolence poems for the death of family members, no wedding poems, no congratulations on the births of sons. Most critics have found

his three or four conventional compliments to Augustus's program encouraging the stability of the Roman household and
family to be the flattest and least inspired of his patriotic verses.
Some of the great human experiences and passions were closed
off to Horace by the same devotion to success and self-advance-
ment that took him so far in Roman society while still so young,
and that filled the roll of his friends with nobles of the old
regime and great men of the new. It may be that Horace the man
really was fortunate to find at the top, in Maecenas, a man
nearly as unattached and quite as unconventional as himself, on
whom he could discharge some of the emotions he felt for his
father, and might have felt for a son. Certainly it was to
Maecenas, as the addressee of poems, that Horace directed, in
full consciousness of the anomaly, his versions of the commonplace topics and phrases that other ancient poets thought
suitable for addressees who could be labeled "family members"
or "long-term loves."

So much for the "real" Horace of 65–30 B.C.; the rest of his
biography, from Octavian's return to Rome in 29 B.C. and his
triumph over Cleopatra and Antony to Horace's death in 8 B.C.,
can be left till later. Horace's poetry falls into periods that have
distinct characteristics. The young Horace of the triumviral period, of the *Satires* and *Epodes*, is a poet well worth considering for
himself alone.

II HORACE BEFORE AUGUSTUS

The Satires

The first book of poems Horace published, in 35 or perhaps as early as late 36, is a set of ten satires (in Latin *sermones,* "familiar discourses"). The *Satires* are intended as an exemplary reworking of the manner of a Roman Republican classic which survives only in fragments, the satires of Lucilius (ca. 180–02 B.C.). Horace professes to consider these brilliant, clever, and for their time even learned but wordy, formless, and self-indulgent: as though the relation between himself and Lucilius as satirists was like that in English literature between the harsh couplets of Donne's satires and the flawless verses of Pope's a hundred years later. In actuality, the reputation of Lucilius as a poet stood quite high both before and after Horace. Horace mitigates these criticisms a little in his second book, and since nearly every one of his own satires is a redoing of some Lucilian theme that implies arduous study of the original, we have a right to think that his denigration of Lucilius is in part an assumed stance in favor of exacting literary art, rather than an expression of real contempt.

In any event, Horace is not merely imitating but presenting himself as the Lucilius of his age. Lucilius stood high in the noble circles that patronized literature in his day, and praised his patrons and friends, though with much freedom of speech; Horace can imply that his familiarity with Maecenas's circle is like Lucilius's with such great men as his patrons Laelius and Scipio. Lucilius's poetry made him so important a public figure that he was given a state funeral when he died, though he was only an eques and had held no public office. Horace throughout his poetry claims a similar prominence for himself in the Roman world. Lucilius practiced all the forms that Horace uses in the

Satires: dialogue, anecdote, autobiographical pieces, and philosophical "diatribes" against various forms of human folly. The Roman *sermo* or satire as Lucilius established it was a wider genre than the word *satire* suggests today, and it remained so. But Lucilius's sexual frankness and realistic portrayal of the lowlife of his day were in fact accompanied by much frank, daring, and personal political satire. "He castigated the people's leaders and the people tribe by tribe," Horace says admiringly of him (*Satires* 2.1.69). But here Horace could not imitate him. Horace does indeed "satirize" numerous contemporaries by name, but not the truly powerful. Moreover, unlike Juvenal, who says frankly that in his day it is safer to satirize the dead than the living, Horace does not confront this question quite head-on in his otherwise excellent apologias for his art in his programmatic satires. One could call this a want of courage, but it is not entirely that. Horace's whole life and work imply that the raucous political warfare of the grandees and gangs of the free Republic, amid which he grew up, was nothing that he and his class, particularly after Philippi, wanted to revive.

Horace probably took up the genre of satire after joining Maecenas's circle in 38. If so, the poems were written over a relatively short period of time. It seems beyond doubt, at any rate, that the ten poems belong together in something like the way the pieces in one of Bach's or Handel's suites belong together. Like the pieces in a suite, each can also be considered separately as a whole, and they are of similar but not equal length. The analogy with the suite also holds in the sense that we are supposed to listen to the component pieces in order. The first three poems, a closely organized set of moral discourses, and satires 1.4, 1.5, and 1.6—three autobiographic pieces which carry on with themes laid out in satires 1.1–3, using Horace as their exemplar—are all between 100 and 150 lines long. Satires 1.7, 1.8, and 1.9 are a set of shorter anecdotal pieces, 35, 50, and 78 lines long, respectively. Satire 1.10, a tailpiece which offers itself explicitly as a resolution to some questions proposed earlier in the book and especially in satire 1.4, returns to the longer model (92 lines). We know that books of poems had been arranged in this striking and thought-provoking form at least since the days of the Greek poets of Hellenistic Alexandria two and a half centuries earlier. The second book of eight satires, published in 31 or 30, and the book of twenty epistles that Horace published later in life, are also in this suite form.

If we take this description of the form of the *Satires* for granted and begin at the first satire, we would still be at a loss without a note on how the genre called *satura* worked in Roman poetry. The subject is avarice. The poem falls elegantly into three parts, each of which is echoed in the next two satires. All the first three poems have (a) a twenty- to twenty-five-line prologue, the first one arguing that men are lying when they wish their occupation in life were different; (b) a body which suggests that some mean can be reached between extremes, in this case between avarice or miserliness and the life of the showy wastrel; and (c) a ten- to fifteen-line conclusion, in this case a fairly subtle one; that the wish for a different life or occupation is merely a cover for insatiable greed, the real disease of both miser and wastrel. Contentment, not so much with one's occupation in life as with the *extent* of one's resources, is the remedy. This sounds sedate enough, especially compared to Juvenal's spectacular attack on contemporary vices in his first satire, and perhaps a translation of the prologue will not at first make the reader eager for more:

> Why is it, Maecenas, that no one lives content
> with the life his plans or his luck provided, but
>   praises
> different lives? The soldier heavy with years,
> arthritic with labor, envies the fortune of merchants;
> but the merchant, as the seawinds tear at his ship,
> cries, "I'd rather be a soldier; in a single moment
> they clash and it's over, quick death or they've won,
>   they're rich."
> The legal consultant praises the life of farmers
> when, the moment the cock crows, clients beat at his
>   door;
> but the farmer, dragged under penalty to a lawcase
> in the city, cries that the good life's only in Rome.
> These antitheses could be carried on at such length
> it would tire even Fabius's tongue. Not to tire *you*,

here is my point: If a God were to say, "Behold me,
I am here to grant wishes: you who were once a
    soldier
are now a merchant; who were once a lawyer, a
    farmer.
Change roles and off with you all to your new lives.
    Hey!
Why stand there?" they *wouldn't*—and yet they
    could—be happy.
What reason for Jupiter not to puff both his cheeks
in rage and swear that hereafter he'll be less easy
in hearing prayers? Besides, not to toss this off like a
    giggling
joker—though really, why shouldn't the truth be told
with a smile, as teachers give boys alphabet cookies
to coax them into learning their alphabet—
but away with jokes, let's be wholly serious now.

[Satires 1.1.1–27]

I might be thought here to have given Horace away: he *is*
the monger of tranquil moral commonplaces whose bland "satirical" verse is so much less inviting than Juvenal's. In reality,
both the giddy movement of the thoughts and the flat com-
monplaceness of each one are brilliant tricks. What Horace is
taking for imitation and reworking first of all, then, is a genre
that encouraged Lucilius to be at his most garrulous and formless, the philosophical "diatribe," the ancestor of the Christian
sermon. This genre—like many others common in Roman satire, for example, the autobiographical narrative and the invitation to a dinner or wine party—combines comic and satirical
elements with others that we would not class as satirical, in this
case, serious or semiserious exhortation to virtue and good
behavior.

We know both from earlier fragments and from preserved
complete works by writers later than Horace (Seneca, Epictetus,
Marcus Aurelius) that diatribe literature had accumulated long
before Horace a body of conventional topics, themes, and arguments. Originality consisted mostly in adding one's own lights of
style and genius, or just new illustrations, to a sentence or para-

graph of serious or satiric exhortation whose paraphrasable content was already familiar. The conventions of the genre include
an addressee or audience, singular or plural (like Maecenas in the
example above). But there is also much recounting of moral
anecdotes about, or sayings of, various exemplary men, wicked
or wise, some of them quite homely:

> A man of rank was coming out of a brothel;
> Cato's heaven-sent wisdom told him, "Well done, my
> boy!
> For when lust poisons your veins, young men like
> you
> are right to come down here, and not stick it straight
> to other men's wives."   [*Satires* 1.2.31–35]

Also, the arguments can be directed at mythical or anonymous imaginary objectors who enter at random for no purpose
except to be answered:

> Agamemnon, why do you forbid the burial
> of Ajax? "I'm king." I'm poor; I give up. "But it's
> right,
> what I ordered! But if someone thinks it unjust,
> he may tell me his thoughts scot-free." Oh greatest of
> kings,
> may the gods let you capture Troy and bring the ships
> home.
> Will you really engage in question and answer with
> me?   [*Satires* 2.3.187–92]

This is why in the example above Maecenas—who, if not
very contented, hardly needed reproving for either avarice or
wanting to be someone else—is by no means the same person as
the "you" Horace addresses at any given point in the poem. The
reference to the mercilessly wordy Stoic preacher "Fabius" is
inserted on purpose to indicate that the genre is indeed diatribe,
and that as practiced *by anyone so far but Horace*, Lucilius included, it is formless and random enough.

Fabius's name, or that of another real or imaginary Stoic
sermonizer-at-length named Crispinus, appears here and there
in each of the first four satires for this purpose. It is one of a
number of thematic devices that indicate that the opening

poems are a coherent group. In *Satires* 1.1, by the simple three-part form he has imposed, Horace gives the reader from the start a sample of the form that his hexameter poetry will perfect: a logic of transition that imitates the free form of conversation by its quick, apparently unconnected transitions of thought, but always repays the reader with a sense of progression and coherent argument in the end. By the use of this subtle "conversational logic," Horace manages to fit his *sententiae* and his illustrations, short (a line or a few words) or long (a paragraph or verse), into perfect and subtle coherence:

> the ant, that little model for great labors   [line 33]

> A limit to seeking wealth! When you have enough
> and poverty's less of a terror, begin to limit
> your labors, now you have what you lusted for; or
> you'll be like a certain Ummidius. The story's short.
> Rich, numbering his drachmas in bushels, and
>   scummy enough
> that he never outdressed his own slaves, to the end of
>   his life
> he feared to starve. His floozy freedwoman split him
> in half with an ax—magnificent Clytemnestra!
>   [92–100]

> When I forbid you avarice, I do not
> encourage you to become a wastrel and spendthrift:
> . . . .
> there's a middle way in things, there are certain limits
> beyond which, within which, right cannot consist.
>   [103–07]

Or, as Pope translates one of Horace's many repetitions of this concept, the recurrent theme not only of the first triad of satires but of many further satires and poems:

> Between Excess and Famine lies a mean,
> Plain, but not sordid, tho' not splendid, clean.
>   [*Satires* 2.2.47–48]

And so Horace comes to his elegant conclusion, subtly twisting together avarice, spendthriftiness, and discontent. A person who pretends he wants to be someone else is merely concealing his own greed, his forgetting of self-realization, enjoyment, and affection for friends and family for the rat race of acquiring more. For any such person could stop now, enjoy himself in moderation, and be himself. Then he would envy no one. Horace draws this conclusion in a spectacular double closure (a thought from Lucretius and who knows how many before, about leaving life like a contented guest, and a self-referential triumph over the formless messiness of "Crispinus" and Lucilius):

> We are back where I started: it's greed that makes everyone
> dispraise his own life and value those of others.
> Because another man's goat drags heavier udders,
> he wastes away and will not compare himself
> with the greater throng of worse-off; wears himself out
> to outdo this man and that. But for all his hustling
> there's always a richer man in the way; as when
> a rush of hooves takes chariots out at the races,
> the charioteer pushes after the horses ahead
> and forgets the man he left in the ruck. That's why
> so rarely we can discover a man who tells us,
> "My life has been happy. I'm content with the days gone by,
> and I leave like a guest who enjoyed the feast to the full."
> Now *that* is enough: you'll think I've rifled the desk
> of bleary Crispinus himself: not a word more.
>
> [108–21]

It is usually said of Beethoven's dry, brilliant Triple Concerto on the record sleeves that the cleverness of its form is somewhat wasted on the tuneless, uninteresting themes. Aristotelian-Epicurean Moderation in the Pursuit of Wealth, treated with this economy and elegance, might seem at first to deserve the same criticism. Horace is doing something more brilliant, however. He has set the three-part form and the maxim *est modus in rebus* ("there's a middle way in things") in the reader's mind by using a relatively unexciting theme to demonstrate the form of the next pieces, without overwhelming form and theme at first in glare and additional subtleties. That can come next. He plans to treat Moderation in Sex Life (part 2) as a portrait of the diatribist— himself—as a raw young Roman hellion of few or occasional scruples, and only "moderate" about sex insofar as he is afraid of trouble. He plans to treat Moderation in Friendship (part 3) as a surprisingly frank picture of his attempts to live up to Maecenas and his circle, in which the "you" of the diatribe and the addressee, Maecenas the Rich Friend, are for once close to the same, and the speaker is both the preacher and Horace the Humble Friend. The generalizations come down to earth, and to cases, in spectacular style in these poems.

   The second poem begins with a prologue of similar shape to the first:

> The Syrian flute-girls' guild, the venders of charms,
>   beggar-priests, mimes, bath attendants, display their
>   grief,
> their public sorrow: Tigellius the singer's dead,
> and a soft touch is gone! But here's a fellow so stingy
>   that
> sooner than be called a spendthrift, he'd let a poor
>   friend
> freeze and starve. Ask the one why he swilled away
> his father's and grandfather's wealth on himself; why
>   he paid
> every day for dinner at usury; he'd tell you *he* won't
> be talked of as mean and small-souled. Some like his
>   spirit.
> Some don't. Fufidius fears to be talked of as
>   spendthrift
> and wastrel, rich as he is in lands and accounts
> at interest; knifing out 60 percent a year;
> the sillier his client is, the higher the rakeoff.
> His favorite accounts are tiros new to the toga,
> brought up by harsh fathers.   [*Satires* 1.2.1–17]

This promising antithesis, so much like that in the first prologue and yet so unlike it, is supposed to be summed up in a
deduction that Tigellius and Fufidius have one thing in common: they both miss the mean recommended in the first poem.

> When fools avoid vice, they run to the contrary vice.
> Maltinus's tunic trails on the ground; another
> is so elegant, girds it so high, he becomes a flasher.
>
> [24-26]

Here the prologue ends and the application, to the world of
Roman sex-life, begins. Theoretically, the application is this:
some refuse to sleep with anybody but high-born society ma-
trons (lines 28-29), some refuse to sleep with anybody but a
prostitute "on exhibit in a stinking whorehouse" (30). But there
is a middle way, which Horace introduces with a low pun:
"How much safer your load [*merx*, merchandise, investment] is
in the class [*classis*, fleet] between; freedwomen, I mean" (47f.).
Freedwomen made safe mistresses, because a Roman of rank
could not be expected to marry one or make her his heir. So that,
logically, and if the world were sensible, young Romans would
eschew both expensive adultery with noblewomen and cheap
slave prostitutes, and take freedwomen concubines who were
citizens but safely below their class.

But the middle road in this case is not so simple, since one
can go as crazy about freedwomen as about any other women
(48-63). Horace therefore revises his middle term. A fairly
pricey prostitute or kept woman (or boy) would be the middle
term between matron and "stinking whore," or the still easier
satisfaction of raping one of one's own slaves.

> Villius thought he could call himself Sulla's son-in-law
> with Fausta. Deceived by the glory, he got only pain
> and too much of it: beaten with fists, chased with
>   sharp steel,
> shut out of doors, with Longarenus fawning inside.
> If his soul could speak for his prick, beholding such
>   evil,
> it would say, "What do you want? Did I ever demand
> a consular, nay, a dictatorial cunt

> wrapped in a matron's white stole, when I got all
>   burning and stiff?
> What could he answer? "A great man's daughter's my
>   girlfriend"?   [64–72]

Horace's talking penis is apparently unique in ancient poetry,
although Lucilius (fragment 237) had been gross enough to picture one weeping.

"Nature" is simple in her demands; many a prostitute is
better looking than society women:

> "Hunters chase after hares
> in deep snow, but won't touch what's all too easily
>   caught,"
> the poet sings, adding, "My love is like that, skips
>   over
> what's there to be had, and chases whatever shuns
>   it."
> ....
> But when thirst burns your jaws, do you wait for cups
> of gold? Or, hungry, do you disdain all food
> but peacocks and Dover sole? When your cock is
>   swollen
> and here's a slave, maid, or houseboy, whom you can
>   grab
> right now, would you rather burst with the itch?
>   Not I.
> What I love is sex you can have on the spot, and
>   simply.
> Leave Mrs. "Later," "More-Money," "If-My-
> Husband's-Out"
> to the eunuchs.   [96–121]

The poet quoted is Callimachus, the model poet's poet of
Hellenistic times, who had used the pursuit of the recherché
and elegant in love as an image of the poet's similar ideal in
literary matters. Satire requires a more moderate ideal. The contemporary Epicurean philosopher and epigrammatist Philodemus of Gadara, a great favorite of Horace's circle, offered a good
description, and his ideals in poetry were as elegant and slender
as Callimachus's own:

So Philodemus says, and takes, for himself,
a not-too-pricey girl who comes when she's told—
no waffling; fair-skinned, straight-bodied, made up
    enough
to look no more white and tall than nature has made
    her.
When I've got the left side of her body under my
    right,
she's my mythical Roman goddess and nymph, any
    name
will do then . . . .   [121–26]

With a prostitute, Horace argues, you're not afraid that her
husband will return and pandemonium break out—which he
brilliantly describes: doors breaking, dogs barking (the Latin
reproduces their grr's by repeated r's: *nec vereor ne dum futuo vir
rure recurrat, / ianua frangatur, latret canis)*:

No fear while I'm fucking that her husband will get
    back from the farm,
the doors will burst in, Rover will bark, everywhere
    great
brouhaha in the house, the woman, whiter than a
    sheet,
will jump up roaring, "I'm ruined, he'll break my
    legs."
She's out to save her dowry, I'm out to save me.
I must flee in a bare tunic and no shoes,
lest I lose my money—or my ass—or my reputation.
Getting caught is an evil: even Fabius has to admit it.
                                                  [130–34]

For a second time Horace concludes with a slam at "Fabius" and
Stoic ethics, which held that only vice is an evil and that pain
and death are indifferent.

Satire 1.3 is about friendship. For a third time Horace opens
with a prologue, this time a brilliant sketch of the crazy Tigellius, recently dead, who was partly characterized in satire
1.2. Now we have not paired human antitheses, but one man
who embraces all antitheses in his one self, the ancestor of many

a "character" in seventeenth- and eighteenth-century satire and even biography:

> Nothing coherent in him: sometimes he'd run
> as if routed by enemies, more often walk pompously
> like a priest of Juno processing. Now he had two
> hundred,
> now a mere ten slaves; now he talked kings and
> tetrarchs,
> everything grand, now "only a three-footed table
> for me, a shell of white salt, a toga that's coarse
> but keeps off the cold." If you gave a hundred
> thousand
> to this sparing, contented person, within five days
> his coffers were empty; he'd sit up to the break of
> dawn
> and snore the whole day; nothing was ever so
> different
> from its own self.   [*Satires* 1.3.9–19]

The "unequal" person who is the subject of the satire's main part now turns out to be the person who is, on the one hand, lenient enough to forgive himself anything, but is, on the other hand, a harsh, unforgiving critic of the vices of a friend. The middle term, the *modus*, here would be to recognize one's own minor vices with humility and make the same excuses for those of friends (lines 21–36). That harsh critics of everyone but themselves are bad friends is a familiar commonplace of the diatribe. But Horace's way of developing this commonplace is to revive Maecenas, whose name has not appeared in the book since its opening, as addressee, and Horace himself personally as the speaker. He does this first only distantly and implicitly; he uses the impersonal "you" that the diatribe-speaker uses to his audience, but the examples given all involve objections that Horace makes elsewhere, or represents Maecenas as making, to himself:

> You're blear-eyed, use no ointment, in viewing your
> faults;
> why, then, do you see your friends' vices as sharply

as an eagle, a glaring snake? But the opposite
happens to you when they criticize you back.
Here's one, a bit hasty-tempered, too loud-mouthed
for these elegant critics. He can be laughed at: his
     toga
is as lopshaped as his haircut, the wrong-sized shoe
flops on his feet. But he's a fine man, the finest
you know; he's your friend, and great artistic genius
hides in that messy body.   [25-34]

Horace tells us elsewhere (for example, at *Satires* 1.5.30) that he
had a recurrent eye infection which he treated assiduously with
ointments; in these lines he transfers his own eye infection to
Maecenas, or just the impersonal "you," as a metaphor for the
blindness of the wealthy and powerful friend to his own faults,
and recommends that "you" imitate him in seeking treatment.
On the other hand, Horace represents himself throughout his
poems as hasty-tempered, and as inclined to resent Maecenas's
perpetual criticisms of his dress and appearance. So the rest of
this sly passage is undoubtedly meant to be taken as a self-
portrait of Horace, the messy young genius of a client.

     Now shake yourself down,
find whether Nature has sown any faults in you,
or perhaps some tiny bad habit, even? For truly
the cabbage fern grows long roots in ungardened
     fields.
And here let us notice that the ugly points of a
     mistress
escape the blind lover; may even delight him, as
     Hagne's
polyp delights Balbinus. I wish that in friendship
we would err the same way, that Wisdom herself
     might have given
an honest name to the error. As a father does not
scorn a son's bad points, so neither should friends:
A father calls his boy Roguish if he has a squint, or
his Puppy if he's as dwarfish as poor abortive
Sisyphus . . . .   [34-47]

Paetus ("roguish") and Strabo ("squint-eyed") were both
Roman nobles' names (Pullus, "puppy," is also attested), and
Sisyphus was a dwarf jester of Mark Antony's, presumably still
alive in 35 B.C. The point of this argument is that it reproduces a
famous topos from Lucretius (*On the Nature of Things* 4.1136ff.)
about how *lovers*, not friends or fathers, give various pet names to
their mistresses', not friends' or childrens', various faults and
blemishes. Lucretius's passage is itself reproduced from Plato's
Republic (474d), and probably the commonplace was picked up
even by Plato from the sophists or the Old or Middle comic stage.
The transformation is intentional: Horace's friendship with
Maecenas, as we saw earlier, takes the place in his poetry of both
"long-term love relationship" and "family relationship."

> Is he a loudmouth, boastful? Let's call him "forward
> and chatty with friends." Too frank and truculent?
> Praise his "courageous honesty." Hot-tempered?
> Call him "spirited." I think that makes men friends
> and keeps them such; but we take even their virtues
> and turn them over, stain the clean cup
> with dregs.
> . . . .
>   If a man's straightforward,
> as I've often and freely shown myself to you,
> Maecenas; if he talks when a friend's reading
> or thinking: "Troublesome character," we say,
> "Lacks the sense God gave him." Alas, how
>   thoughtlessly
> we legislate unfairness against ourselves!
>   [49–56, 63–67]

If we appreciate that Horace has been talking about himself
and Maecenas all through the satire, the appearance of Maecenas's name so late, revealing the identity of "you," is exquisite.
So are some of the offences Horace pretends to think a friend
should be forgiven as minor:

> He got drunk and pissed on the dinner couch;
> dropped from the table

a cup once held in ancient Evander's hands.
For this, or because he got hungry and grabbed some
    chicken
from my part of the platter, is he less my amusing
    friend?
What would I do if he stole, or betrayed my secrets,
or defaulted on loans? A Stoic says all faults are equal;
reality puts him in trouble. Both feelings and practice
refute him, as does the mother of justice and equity—
Convenience.   [90–98]

Horace now (once more imitating Lucretius, 5.1092ff.) gives
a mock history of the social contract, from the days when men
lived on acorns and battled like beasts. Not Nature but Convenience led men to social life and the forbidding of theft, brigan-
dage, and (shades of satire 2) adultery.

For long before Helen, cunt was the fiercest cause
of warfare; yet theirs were but nameless deaths
whom the stronger man, the bull of the herd, laid
    low,
as they fought for random sex in the manner of
    beasts.   [107–10]

So this time the mean of good and reasonable behavior is
established—as the Epicureans would have agreed—by the social contract and by reason, not by Nature, as in the first two
satires. Men simply learned to treat each others' faults lightly by
experience and by convenience. Nature and our bodies teach us
moderation in seeking property, which is merely seeking food
and shelter, and in sex; but our highest part, our intellect, must
balance out friendship. Horace is making no mistake in ordering
property, sexuality, and friendship on the ascending scale of
intensity $1:2:3$, where a romantic poet might want it to be
$1:3:2$. All his poems imply this scale of values—that of an
unmarried and romantically uncommitted man. And now he
can have for the third time his epilogue, with, for the third time,
the Stoics for his butt. Since another Stoic paradox was that
"only the wise man is king, and all fools are slaves," Horace
triumphantly concludes:

Let me cut this short: you go to your penny
    bathhouse,
King, with no train to attend you except for silly
Crispinus. But I have indulgent friends to forgive me
my foolish errors, and I as willingly bear with
their delinquencies in turn. So I, a plebeian,
live in more joy than such kings can ever know!

[137–42]

I have treated the opening triad of satires, and particularly
this happy poem, at more length than I shall the others, because
they show so clearly that Horace's informal poems conceal as
perfect a sense of form as the greatest of his odes. In addition,
one ought to say of the third satire that it is one of the most
beautiful poems of friendship ever written. *Amicitia* in Latin
implies not mere friendship but acting together, and there is no
doubt that in choosing to write this way Horace identifies himself as Maecenas's client and companion nor merely in private
life but in his business and political interests; indeed, there is
hardly such a thing to the ancient mind, whether Greek or Roman, as friendship separate from the idea of acting together in
the world. And yet in this subtle expression of protest against
being criticized for small things, in this Aristotelian attempt to
make the lesser and greater friend equal in free speech, there is
more of an image of real friendship than in many of the most
famous documents of male friendship that merely express affection. Horace begins from what he represents as petty criticisms
of himself from Maecenas and his circle. He voices a client's free
resentment at being unjustly put down among them. The impression left, paradoxically, is more intimate and friendly than if
he had merely praised them.

The second triad of satires (there are other ways to group
them, but I believe the most prominent pattern is that which
simply takes them in sequence: 1–3, 4–6, 7–9, 10) begins by
acknowledging Horace's great predecessor in the genre, Lucilius. The comic poets of Athens satirized real persons in their
city with great freedom.

Lucilius is like them entirely; he follows them;
he changes only the feet and rhythm; a genius,

> an elegant critic, but a rough composer of verse.
> For that was his vice: two hundred verses an hour
> he dictated (what a hero!) while he stood on one leg.
> He flowed like a muddy river; you would wish to
>   cancel
> much; a lazy, garrulous craftsman at writing,
> or writing well—I concede that he wrote a *lot*.
>
>   [*Satires* 1.4.6–13]

Horace meant these lines as attention-getters: Lucilius was still much admired, indeed the standard model for political and personal satire in verse. This bold announcement that Horace meant not just to take up the genre but to reform it is followed by a characteristically unexpected development of the argument. "Crispinus" can write as many verses as he pleases; Horace's verses are not for the mob, but not because of their fineness, as one would expect him to say after this beginning. The image of the muddy river (as opposed to the pure spring of fine writing) is a pointed quotation from Callimachus (ca. 280 B.C.), the great archetype of the Alexandrian "learned" and bookishly elegant poet. But instead of complimenting himself on his own Alexandrian elegance, Horace takes that for granted and goes on to claim instead that he recites little in public because not only personal but even general satire is risky and unpopular to write. Here he tacitly concedes that his examples of objects of satire from "real life," unlike the fearless Lucilius's, are mainly either minor characters in society (people of his own rank or near it) or fictitious, or from the previous generation and even earlier. Never mind; even a general sermon is "dangerous":

> Take anyone right from the crowd:
> he's troubled and turbid with greed or wretched
>   ambition.
> This one's on fire for brides and that one for boys;
> the splendor of silver for this one; old bronzes for
>   Albius.
> This one's a merchant and sails from the rising sun
> to the warmth of sunset, driven headlong through
>   danger
> like dust in a whirlwind, fearing to lose his fortune

or just wanting more. All these are afraid of
    lampoons,
will have nothing to do with poets. "Hay's on his
    horns:
get out of his way! As long as he raises a laugh
he won't spare his best friend. Whatever he scrawls
    on his page
he shows everyone at every fountain and breadshop,
boys and old women included." But come: let me
    speak for myself.
First: might I exclude myself from those I accept
as poets? Don't say it's enough to put it in verse . . . .

[25–41]

Now Horace takes up the question of poetic technique he had
raised earlier. He asks whether poetry like his and Lucilius's can
be poetry at all, being as it is *sermoni propiora*, "too like talk." So
also some wonder whether comedy is poetry, since apart from
the meter any angry father of a wastrel might talk the same Latin
as in a comic play. Neither genre is like epic, which uses a
grander language than normal, and whose words, even put
back in prose order, would still let you see the *disiecta membra*,
the torn-apart limbs, of a poet.

Enough of that; another time we'll consider
if it's poetry or not; now only if you distrust
this kind of writing with justice.   [63–65]

Insofar as Horace is comparing himself with Lucilius, his
own verses are the answer. When Horace does a three-line characterization of "Ummidius," he works over every letter in Ummidius's name to some profit:

Ummidius quidam, non longa est fabula, dives
ut metiretur nummos, ita sordidus ut se
non umquam servo melius vestiret . . . .

[*Satires* 1.1.95–97]

. . . a certain Ummidius. The story's short.
Rich, numbering his drachmas in bushels, and

scummy enough
that he never outdressed his own slaves . . . .

And every apparently simple page of the *Satires* is full of
subtleties of sonic effect that Lucilius hardly dreamed of, as in
the last lines of satire 1.1:

iam satis est; ne me Crispini scrinia lippi
compilasse putes, verbum non amplius addam.

Now *that* is enough: you'll think I've rifled the desk
of bleary Crispinus himself: not a word more.

In Horace even the simplest lines have so much going on,
as here, where one watches with admiration the name *Crispini*
generate *scrinia, lippi,* and *compilasse* out of its consonants and
vowel, and the first word of the couplet, *iam,* is perfectly echoed
in *amplius addam.* That was why it was so clever of him to quote
Callimachus, the great Alexandrian master of laborious, learned
verse-music, against Lucilius. But Horace's theory of *how* to write
such verses must wait until satire 1.10 at the end of the book.

On the other question he raised, whether satire is an un-
social or antisocial act, Horace has another difference from Lucilius to discuss, and here he intends deliberately to explain
himself as less daring. The new Lucilius of Maecenas's circle,
Horace implies significantly, writes in a more tranquil and less
controversial milieu, and applies his lessons to himself as well as
others. For what follows is the picture quoted in chapter 1, of
Horace's father instructing him to learn virtue and vice from
watching how other people's doings go down with their audience, and Horace still pleasantly drawing up such pictures for
the instruction not of the many, but of the few:

It's just one of my minor vices
that I confess to. And, if you won't indulge it,
a regiment of poets* will come to my aid
(we are many too many for you) and like a mob
of Jews will make you give in and join the crowd.
[139–43]

---

*Which already implies, by the way, that the earlier question solves itself:
satiric poets *are* poets and their poems are poetry.

The other autobiographical and anecdotal satires that follow maintain this self-confident tone and perfectly illustrate the literary principles that Horace has laid down. For examples we may look briefly at the two concluding satires, 1.9 and 1.10. The ninth satire is an encounter with an ambitious and talkative literary person, as Horace walks the streets in the innocent peregrinations described in satire 1.6. Horace is too good-natured to get rid of him, and it soon turns out that the bore's real purpose is to crash Maecenas's circle.

> "How do you and Maecenas get on?"
> he put in. "A man with few equals. What a mind.
> No one's managed his luck so well. You'd have a
>   great helper,
> one who can play second fiddle, if you'd present
> your humble servant to him. I'm damned if you
>   wouldn't
> clear rivals out of your way." "But in his house we
>   don't live
> the way you think. No great man's house is more
>   innocent,
> more alien to such unpleasantness; no one can hurt
>   me
> by being richer or cleverer. Each of us has
> his own place." "Great; hardly believable." "Well,
> that's how it is." "You make me burn to be closer
> to him." "You have only to wish."   [*Satires* 1.9.43–54]

A friend wickedly refuses to help Horace get rid of the bore, but an opponent of the bore's in the law courts catches him up right out of the street for the trial; "thus Apollo saved me."

By this firm declaration of the powerful and praiseworthy circle to which he belongs, Horace introduces the tenth and last poem, which opens by taking up where the fourth left off:

> Why yes, I said Lucilius's verses ran
> on careless feet. Who admires Lucilius so blindly
> as not to confess it? But because he rasped the whole
>   city

> with his salty wit, he's praised for the same pages.
> He may have that concession from me, not the rest;
>   for logically
> I would have to call vaudeville scripts beautiful
>   poems.
> It isn't enough to split your hearers' jaws
> with a laugh, though that is also a sign of power.
> Be sparing of words, let them run; don't load down
>   the thought
> with ponderous noises that tire the listener. Language
> should be sharp at one point, amuse at another; assert
> the orator here, the poet there, and sometimes
> the sophisticate, who spares his full forces, who
>   lightens
> on purpose his power of talk. For mockery often
> makes a point more strongly and sharply than violent
>   curses.
> Old Comedy's poets succeeded by these techniques;
> imitate them in *that*.   [*Satires* 1.10.1–17]

A brilliant touch, to promise the answer to the question "Can satire be poetry?" in the fourth poem and give it in the tenth! There are still literal-minded Horatian scholars who make the mistake of thinking that satire 1.10 was written as a reply to the criticism Horace incurred for his daring attack on Lucilius in satire 1.4. That misses the point; satire 1.4 promised something that appears only, and at last, here. And that un-Lucilian subtlety is part and parcel of the point Horace is trying to make against Lucilius. Satire *is* poetry, if you take the trouble of writing it: "or writing well—I concede that he wrote a *lot*." In Horace's circle are successful practitioners of other classic genres whom he lists here: Fundanius (comedy), Pollio (tragedy), Varius (epic), and Vergil (pastoral):

> *This* genre, which Varro of Atax (and some others)
> tried in vain, was what I found I could write best,
> though not as well as its founder; nor would I dare to
>   tear off
> the crown that clings to his brow, nor the great
>   praise.   [lines 46–49]

Didn't Lucilius laugh at Ennius's clunky verses,
though he hardly thinks himself greater than him he
condemns? [54–55]

May Plotius and Varius, Maecenas and Vergil
together,
Valgius Rufus, and my good Octavian approve this,
may Fuscus and both the Visci give me applause;
You, Pollio, and you, Messalla, with your brother,
together
with Bibulus, Servius, and you, most generous
Furnius,
and others, my learned friends and comrades, whose
names
I need not parade. Whatever these verses are worth,
I should like to please you; will be hurt if they fail my
hope.
Demetrius, you and Tigellius go indulge in
a good cry on your chairs in front of your schoolgirl
pupils.
Go, slave, and write this in at the end of my book.
[81–92]

So Horace fulfills another promise he made in satire 1.4: he
does have his "cloud of witnesses," his crowd of poets to cry
down the critics, and not only poets of all stripes, but also
Maecenas and a brilliant visitors' list of great literary and political noblemen of both Octavian's party and Antony's. As for
Demetrius and Tigellius (probably the son of the man satirized
in poems 1.2 and 1.3), like the poets Pope made fun of in the
Dunciad, they mainly exist because Horace mentioned them.

The book, taken as a whole, is one of the most joyous in
Latin literature; what dark thoughts it hints at only throw its
brightness into greater prominence. It is a continuous celebration of social success, of friendship, of conscious poetic talent
exercised for a circle who understand and respect it, of self-
realization and self-confidence. Only those who think consciously or unconsciously that "poetry" must be like the "Ode
on a Grecian Urn," and that talking penises and mock sermons,
pointed analyses of political friendships, literary journeys with

influential statesmen, and imaginary autobiography "ought" not to belong to high literature, could fail to be impressed by it. The second book of *Satires* is mainly in dialogue form, contrasted with the diatribe form used for most of the first book. The eight poems are arranged unmistakably, like those in the first book, on a plan. One major theme is the presentation of a Horace who is still more assured of his success by Maecenas's recent gift of the Sabine farm. This expensive piece of country property, with its five prosperous tenant farms, was outside Tibur in the northwest, near Sabine country, on the edge of the fashionable senatorial belt of country retreats twenty or thirty miles from Rome. We need not take literally Horace's descriptions of his farm as the humble seat of moderation. He was clearly overwhelmed with pleasure in it; it figures in satires 2.3 and 2.7, and is the main subject of satire 2.6, a formal poem of thanks to Maecenas. Expressions of gratitude recur in the *Epodes, Odes,* and *Epistles.* (None of Horace's other poems thanks anyone explicitly for a gift or a favor, though Augustus later in life conferred two large gifts on Horace, one of which was probably a house in Tibur itself, which Suetonius saw.) But the idyllic description of his life on retreat in satire 2.6 has occupied too much critical attention, as though Horace professed to be already retiring there at thirty-five from a city life that still clearly excited him to the core. Satires 2.7 and 2.8 sharply undercut satire 2.6 by revealing a Horace still deeply engaged in Roman pleasures and in the politics and dinner parties of Maecenas's circle.

Other themes clearly emerge from book 2: satire 2.1 is about the dangers of writing personal satire, and satire 2.5, the most Juvenalian of Horatian satires, is a fearsomely brilliant skit on the greed and shamelessness of legacy hunters (Ben Johnson borrowed from it for *Volpone*). In satire 2.3 the Stoic convert Damasippus invades the Sabine farm and "proves" to Horace that he is a hypocrite and fool; in satire 2.7 Horace's own slave Davus, who has learned the diatribe style from "Crispinus's janitor," confronts him with even worse criticisms. So the odd-numbered satires are somehow parallel, 2.1 corresponding to 2.5 and 2.3 to 2.7. Satires 2.2, 2.4, 2.6, and 2.8 also have a theme:

the social anthropology of Roman dining—country (old-fashioned, simple, ancestral Roman) dining in satires 2.2 and 2.6, city (new-fangled, pretentious, arriviste) dining in satires 2.4 and 2.8. Satire 2.2 is a lecture that Horace ascribes to a virtuous Roman bourgeois who believes that the unattractive cuisine of his generation, adhered to on his farm, is more conducive to health and the practice of virtue than modern kickshaws. Satire 2.4, in complete contrast, deals with the elegances of prosperous triumviral Rome's nouvelle cuisine; a young Epicurean expert lectures Horace on what he recommends as fine, but not pompous, dining. Satire 2.6, after thanking Maecenas for the Sabine farm and describing Horace's exhausting but pleasurable business life in Rome, concludes with Horace having an old-fashioned patriarchal dinner at his country retreat among his slaves, tenant farmers, and neighbors, and listening happily to the fable of the Town Mouse and the Country Mouse. Satire 2.8, again in contrast, depicts Horace listening with eager and malicious joy as a fellow member of Maecenas's circle describes to him the total failure of a dinner by which a pretentious bore, able to talk about nothing but his own recipes, had hoped to push himself in among them.

The arrangement of the first book of satires, in short, commands one to read the poems in order; that of the second adds a clear admonition to compare certain poems. Take as examples the three poems that end the second book, satires 2.6–8. The sixth satire is the famous poem of thanks for the Sabine farm:

> This was my prayer: a modest measure of farmland,
> a constant fountain of water near the farmhouse,
> and a bit of forest with it. But the gods have dealt.
> more richly with me and better still. It's enough;
> Mercury, son of Maia, I can pray for nothing
> but that you should make this gift truly my own.
> I never increased my wealth by scheming and
>   malice,
> and will never diminish it by folly, greed, or guilt.
> . . . .
> This present joy suffices me, this is my prayer:

Make my sheep fat, make the whole farm fat, one
   thing
excepted: my slender genius. Protect me as greatly,
Lord, as you have till now!   [1–7, 13–15]

The Sabine farm is already here, as it is in Horace's later
poetry, a symbol of the writer's private self (in contrast to what he
is in the city) and of the "slender genius" of his poetry. The wish
that all should be fat in the countryside except the "slender"
(Greek *lepton*, "delicate, elegant") genius of the poet is, again, an
allusion to Callimachus, like the comparison in *Satires* 1.4 of the
muddy river and the pure stream. The rest of the poem depends
on the contrast between Horace's busy, unpoetic (but cheerful)
day in crowded Rome (quoted in chapter 1) and his peaceful
thoughts in the countryside with his reading and writing and
among his tenants. At a simple country dinner, Horace's neighbor Cervius rebukes a fellow guest for admiring the wealth of
Arellius (another neighbor) with the fable of the Town Mouse
and the Country Mouse. The Country Mouse found that the
splendid feast his disdainful friend showed him in town ended
with the guard dog being set on them (Romans did not use cats
for this purpose), and he departed resolved to live carefree on
vegetables. Of course, this fable undercuts Horace's pleasure in
the Roman business day with its suggestion of the dog-eat-dog
nature of city life. But I am not tempted to dwell on this favorite
passage, as many books on Horace have done; rather, I want to
call attention (once more) to the jarring juxtaposition of this fable,
which ends the sixth satire, with the beginning of the seventh.
One of Horace's town slaves, determined to speak out as slaves
were allowed to do at the Saturnalia, bursts in as unexpectedly in
the opening lines as if he were sick of hearing Horace's hypocritical Country Mouse impersonation in the previous poem. (A
recitation of the book as a whole might have allowed this comic
point to come out.)

"I demand a hearing now! I'm your slave, but I
   wanted
to say what I think, though I'm scared." Davus? "Yes
Davus,

> your loyal property, and honest enough—that's to
>   say,
> for a live human being." All right, then, it's
>   Saturnalia,
> and since our ancestors wanted it so, go on.
> . . . .
> "You praise the simple life of the ancient poor.
> If a god were to lead you to it, you'd turn it down
>   flat,
> because you don't believe your own bellowing lies,
> or because you're too weak to do right, and stuck like
>   a fool,
> your foot in thick mud. Here at Rome you tell us you
>   wish for
> the Sabine farm; there you're a restless farmer
> who praises Rome to the skies."
>
> [*Satires* 2.7.1–5, 22–29]

Romae rus optas: "Here at Rome you wish for the farm." It is
as if Davus is commenting sarcastically on the famous *O rus,
quando ego te aspiciam* ("O my farm, when shall I see you again?")
of the previous poem.

> "If no one invites you
> to dinner, you praise carefree cabbage; as though
> you were dragged to dinners in chains, you thank
>   your stars
> because you needn't get drunk anywhere tonight.
> But Maecenas asks you to dinner just before
>   nightfall—
> you sputter, "Bring me a torch, and quick! Is anyone
> listening, curse it?" Then you're gone straight out the
>   door,
> with Mulvius and your other cheap parasites damning
> *you* as they leave still hungry.   [29–37]

We learn from this that the "humble" poet had humble
clients of his own, cadging dinners from him. Davus offers to
prove, on the authority of "Crispinus's janitor," that Horace is

as much a slave as himself, indeed a cheaper slave than Davus,
who cost a mere two thousand sesterces, and for all his pre-
tenses less of a philosopher, too. It is as if an eighteenth-century
English gentleman were being harangued about religion by a
valet who has been converted by John Wesley's cook. The infection of Stoicism with its theory that only the wise man is king
and all fools are slaves has spread to Horace's own servants.
Horace's clandestine adulteries are less becoming to him than
Davus's simple satisfaction of needs:

> When domineering old Mother
> Nature pushes me on, any woman who's naked
> in the flaring lamplight can take the strokes of my
>   swollen
> hard-on, or use her behind to tickle her horsie
> from above, and send me off, no trouble, no gossip,
> no worries if someone richer or handsomer gets
> his rocks off in the same slit. When you throw off
>   your toga,
> your equestrian ring, and dress up to sneak out at
>   night
> as Dama the slave instead of a wealthy juror,
> a dark wool cloak on your shameless perfumed head,
> aren't you the very thing you're dressed up to be?
>   [47–56]

Davus admits, however, that he has no idea whether
Horace's excursions are for *adultery* (so Horace's morality is
"saved"). He then makes fun of Horace's other upper-class slav-
eries as a gourmet and an art connoisseur, and ends by striking
a strangely poetic and serious note, one that is prophetic of
Horace's lyric vein:

> "You can't spend an hour with yourself, your
>   leisure's a wreck,
> a waste; you're an exile, a runaway slave of your
>   own,
> who tries to put Care off the scent with wine and
>   sleep—

> in vain, for your dark companion is on your heels.
> She follows you, runaway slave!"   [111–15]

Horace's response to these striking lines is remarkable, too:

> "Get me a rock!"
> "For what?" "Nay—arrows!" "The man is insane (or
> a poet)."
> "Get out of here fast, or you'll be the ninth slave I've
> sent
> to dig my ditches out at the Sabine farm!"   [116–18]

Murders, needless to say, were not committed with arrows in Greco-Roman times after the age of epic and tragedy. The two jokes together of course imply—if they imply anything auto-biographical at all—not that Horace inflicted violence on his slaves or sent slaves to the ditches in droves, but that he was used to joking with his slaves about nearly anything. But to threaten a slave with exile to the same Sabine farm that had been such an idyllic retreat in the previous poem is both a fine joke and a paradox that warns us against ever taking Horace's state-ments at surface value.

The grand finale of the book, satire 2.8, is neatly joined to this mock-tragic conclusion, in which a slave is put down for daring to criticize Horace's luxuries. "How did lucky Nasi-dienus's dinner come off, do you think?" Horace asks the comic poet Fundanius as it opens, and he receives a full and very malicious description of its failure, itself a miniature comedy, in reply. The poem seems at least superficially to make out Maecenas's circle as remarkably unamiable people; but a flatly literal interpretation would again be a great mistake. The par-venu Nasidienus Rufus has invited Maecenas and Fundanius to a pretentious gourmet dinner, along with the poets Viscus and Varius, and Maecenas's insolent parasites Vibidius and Balatro. Nasidienus, surrounded on the host's couch by his own flat-terers Nomentanus and Porcius, might have hoped that, if not permitted to crash Maecenas's circle, he would at least be safe from insult. But he discovers to his dismay that he might as well have invited Virginia Woolf, Lytton Strachey, and the rest of the

Bloomsbury group to make fun of his food, his servants, and his manners.

Fundanius the comic poet, appropriately, narrates the dinner to a delighted Horace. Nasidienus, afraid that his expensive Caecuban and Chian wines are not enough, offers Maecenas his choice of Alban or Falernian in addition. Apparently the ancients thought this sort of gesture showy and vulgar, and even worse was a discourse on recipes and gourmandise accompanying dinner. Nasidienus explains that the cold roast boar served with salad for a first course was caught in a mild south wind (that is, it was not too gamy), and that the honey-apples with the entrée were gathered in the waning moon (evidently not only the right thing to do, but a piece of magical superstition which helps justify the reference to the witch Canidia at the end of the poem). This and the rest of his lecture on his own cuisine are rewarded with hostility by his guests and positive insult from Vibidius and Balatro, who swear not to "perish unrevenged" and start chugging down great gulps of his expensive wine before his face. The heavy, dusty dining room curtains collapse all over the entreés in clouds of dirt and plaster, and Nasidienus weeps as if he had lost a son, then goes out pursued by ironical compliments to order a new main course, while his rude guests whisper behind his back. Horace is delighted to hear this:

> I can't imagine a show I'd rather see! Tell me
> what laughs he gave you next. "Vibidius asked
> the waiters if the wine jug broke with the platters,
> since he wasn't getting the wine he ordered. Then he
> quickly pretended with Balatro's help to be laughing
> at something else, as you, oh our host, returned,
> with the face of a hero about to avert disaster
> by his generalship. An enormous platter followed,
> slave-borne, with cut-up roast crane sprinkled with
>   meal
> and salt, with fresh foie gras from a white goose
> fed on figs, and shoulder of hare ('so very much
>   better
> than if it's cooked with the loin,' so we were told),
> and blackened pigeons and doves, breast only too,

delicious stuff if the host hadn't lectured on them,
nature, ingredients, cooking time—we fled after
   dinner [that is, without staying for the obligatory
   wine party],
revenged by skipping the rest, as if Canidia
had puffed over our food her worse-than-serpent's
   breath."   [*Satires* 2.8.79–95]

But the rules of the genre hardly indicate that Maecenas's
circle were such tough critics of food and hosts in real life. One
senses in whatever real situation lay behind the satire some far
more complicated in-joke than we can understand on the basis
of the surviving evidence. Perhaps the joke is purely literary;
Fundanius behaves like a parasite in one of his own (lost) come-
dies, all surface flattery and underhanded sarcasm. All we really
know is that Horace has elegantly completed his theme (old
Roman bourgeois cuisine in satire 2.2; theory of Roman nouvelle
cuisine in satire 2.4; fable of the Town Mouse and the Country
Mouse in satire 2.6; horrors of actual Roman nouvelle cuisine in
satire 2.8) and at the same time drawn a brilliant poetic portrait
of himself at thirty-five, still far too fascinated and amused with
the joys of the city and the excitement and gossip of Rome's
greatest literary and political salon to retire to any country place,
however quiet and beautiful.

The Epodes

The seventeen *Epodes* published in the next year, 29 B.C.,
are a miscellany of love lyrics, political poems, humorous
mimes, satirical attacks, and invectives, ranging from 16 to 203·
lines in length. All but the last, which is in single iambic lines,
are composed in various forms of couplets, mainly based on
iambic and dactylic rhythms. In their greater density and com-
plexity of poetic style, they represent a mid-stage between
Horace's informal hexameter poetry and his lyric poetry, where
the effects become as dense and complex as any in Latin. That is
deliberate, and part of the genre: "iambic" poetry is expected to
be a mid-stage between the informal and the fully "poetic" in
Greek and Latin.

The ethos of the seventeen poems is bright, youthful, self-confident, and imaginative, like that of the *Satires*, and like them learned and allusive. All Horace's poems are immensely broad in their range of literary reference; but the range was altered, the authors Horace took down to restudy in detail changed, with each change of genre. Lucilius, the diatribe-philosophers, and the Greek and Roman comic poets influence the *Epodes* verbally only a little, though Horace was studying them deeply throughout the same period as background for the *Satires*. The genre, style, and metrical form of the *Epodes* bring into Roman poetry for the first time, and very ambitiously, the manner and meter of the great archaic Greek poets Archilochus (seventh century B.C.) and Hipponax (ca. 540 B.C.). Horace takes up their three great subjects: he imitates Archilochus's erotic poetry and war poetry, and Archilochus's and Hipponax's special "iambic" genre of vicious invective. But fragments, translations, and mottoes from them are mixed with and updated by imitations of later Hellenistic poets who had written iambs and erotic elegies and epigrams. In addition, Horace imitates contemporary Roman poets, especially Catullus, who died when Horace was twelve or thirteen. Horace also satirizes his friend Vergil's pastoral and georgic mode to splendid effect in epode 2, but uses it for serious effect in a political piece, epode 16.

Not all the epodes are authoritatively certifiable as great poetry. Some of the poems, especially the pure invectives, seem like practice pieces in technique. Archilochus's invectives are said to have caused suicides, and their fragments certainly sparkle with realistically depicted hate. Some of Horace's invectives are against clearly imaginary opponents, and come off as pure, if vigorous, exercises in genre.

But many other epodes are among Horace's finest and most original work. The first poem is given to Maecenas, who has proposed to accompany Octavian on campaign; and it opens with yet another daring piece of word placement. Maecenas will be on the light ships among great ships of war, and the placement of the word *amice* ("dear one") in line 2 pictures this. My translation is intended to illustrate the epode or long-line, short-line couplet form, in this case one of alternating iambic lines of six and four beats, which is the meter of the first ten epodes:

You'll be on light Liburnian galleys, scudding through
great warships—dear one—high and towered,
prepared, resolved to match Octavian's every risk
with risk, Maecenas, of your own.
And what of me? My life is pleasant
if you're alive; if not, mere pain.

....

I am glad to soldier in this or any war again,
that I may find free grace with you,
not so that, chained to still more oxen, still more
    plows
may tear up still more land for me,
or my Calabrian flocks vacation from the heat
in cool Lucanian pasturelands,
or a new villa gleam high up in Tusculum,
whose grounds adjoin the ancient wall.
Enough, more than enough your great benignity
enriched me, more I cannot use;
I could only bury it, like the miser in a play,
or squander it like a wastrel son.   [*Epodes* 1.1–6, 23–34]

This poem startles a modern reader. It is an effort even for a
professional student of the classics to appreciate its naked, en-
thusiastic presentation of the ethos of patronage and *clientela*; of
"friendship" in a society so explicitly founded on networks of
mutual obligation that to be patron or client (or for very many
men and women, Horace included, both) was as essential as
citizenship and family ties. It was not in any way disgraceful to
be a client, as much Roman poetry shows, but to put up with
insults from a bad patron; not wrong in any way to be a patron,
but to insult clients or fail them; many a rich patron like
Maecenas raised his or her freedmen and clients to the equestrian census and better with gifts. Nor do Horace, or most Roman poets, see anything in the relationship (if it goes well) that
is inconsistent with deep affection. Aristotle's doctrine that services on both sides even out inequality of status and make richer
and poorer friend equal is taken for granted by Horace and by
the Romans in general. The services of client and patron were
not spelled out by moral or legal obligation; they required origi-

nality and thoughtfulness on both sides at every step. A Roman without immediate family, like Horace, could find emotional substitutes in his circle of patrons, clients, and friends more easily than most modern people.

Such thinking echoes through all Horace's poetry to Maecenas. Sometimes the service is as immediate and real as here: joining the patron's staff in wartime. Sometimes it is poetic praise, sometimes a wine party, sometimes wise or humorous advice the humble poet offers to calm the great man's mind, or set him straight amid the temptations and dangers of wealth and power. Equally clear, in both early Horatian satires and late Horatian epistles, is the client's right to complain vigorously of anything degrading in the relationship, or even, as in the third epode, to laugh down his friend for abusing his authority in a trifling matter and making Horace taste a garlic pie. Very purposeful in this poem are the images that make Horace not only an inseparable companion to whom life without Maecenas is tedium, but at once a dove brooding over his friend as chick, and (if he asked for more) a wastrel son of an indulgent father. Tusculum is visible from Rome ("gleam high up in Tusculum"): Horace is not in the least ashamed to point out, even while denying he wants more, that investors in real estate like himself dreamed of property still closer in to Rome than his own. Also, we should note the elegant reference to the standard characters of comedy in the last lines: serious as some of the epodes are, comedy, not tragedy, is the reference point (as in the *Satires*). Horace is already conscious of more ambitious lyric poetry to come, but not in the lighter couplet form of the epodes.

The best-known of all the epodes is the second, "Beatus ille qui procul negotiis." In it are both pervasive comedy and another concentrated portrayal of one of the centerpoints of Roman feeling about life, one easier to grasp than clients and patrons' friendships; the opposition, crucial throughout Horace's poetry, of city/country, business/leisure: *urbs*/*rus*, *otium*/*negotium*. It is pleasant to notice in these last two words that this businesslike people characterized business both in their language and their thought not as a positive value, but as the negation of leisure, *neg*otium. Every Roman man of affairs, from the pushing minor businessmen Horace grew up with to Caesar Augustus himself, conceived of himself, at least for the sake of argument, as a man who longed to leave behind the hectic noise and dirt of Rome and retire to peace, quiet, and the patriarchal life watching the seasons pass in the countryside, and, if he was a literary man, to study poetry and philosophy for their own sakes. The last three satires of book 2, as we saw, are based on the inseparable blend of reality and hypocrisy in this self-conceit that the young Horace felt in himself. Epode 2 crystallizes this peculiarly Roman tension perfectly and for all time. A disembodied voice begins:

> Blessed is he who, far from all these business cares,
> as in the ancient Golden Age,
> can farm his fathers' fields with cattle of his own,
> forgetting about interest rates. [1–4]

The voice imagines itself, in verses of what seems at first pure pastoral beauty, forgetting business and cares in the country. It sees itself marrying vines to ancient poplars; tenderly shearing sheep; grafting fruit trees; sprawled on the grass listening to birds and streams; hunting; forsaking the love affairs of the city for a sunburnt Sabine or Apulian farmwife, of no beauty but great diligence, who will tend its sons, build its fire, milk its farm animals, and strain its wine. Her cuisine will avoid the indigestible luxuries of Rome (which the voice, however, describes at length and with regret even as it condemns them). It will be like a lyric version of Ofellus's Roman country table. What pleasure to be a country mouse and watch, after suitable rural sacrifices, the cattle returning home at night, from a dinner table surrounded by one's own farm-grown slaves! The verses echo with such apparent sincerity the *Eclogues* and *Georgics* of Horace's friend Vergil and their romantic enthusiasm for the countryside and the farm life, that the famous "sting" at the end never loses its point and power:

> When he had reasoned thus, the banker Alfius,
> ready to start his farm right now,

on the ides called in and settled all past due accounts.
He'll lend it on the first again.   [67–70]

Alfius's country enthusiasm lasted only fifteen days, as
brief as Davus in the *Satires* claims was Horace's own enthusiasm for life at the Sabine farm; and meanwhile he had cleared
his books. It is very well to remember Horace as the "lover of
vines and slave to quietness," as Lawrence Durrell called him.
But it is also easy to forget that the Sabine farm was close
enough to Rome and negotium that Horace was hardly in exile
there. He wrote pictures of country life as fine as any of Vergil's,
but preferred the *suburbana*, the fashionable Roman "countryside," with its easily accessible resort towns, not the true
depths of the Italian countryside, which he remembered from
his boyhood. It is probably the elegant sense of placement governing the order of the *Epodes* and *Odes* that makes Horace follow this poem with the third epode, a series of comic curses on
Maecenas for getting him to try a rustic garlic pie. *Cuisine rus-
tique* is not for Horace after all.

The fifth epode, like satire 2.5, is a kind of popular mime. It
is one of a series of four in the book—5, 8, 12, 17—about lustful
old women, a standard genre of Greek and Roman invective,
but one with which Horace had a peculiar fascination. This
theme remains a standard topic in Horace's lyric poetry to the
last, and a most unattractive one. These poems seem, however,
not to fit the kind of feminist study, in terms of male hostility
and fear of female sexuality, that has done so much recently for
the analysis of the mythology and poetry of early Greece. Their
theme seems somehow connected with Horace's life-long refusal of long-term emotional commitments; the old (really only
older) women are a threat to his life-style, the threat, half-
understood, of what Byron called "that household virtue, now
uncommon, / of faithfulness to a bad, ugly woman." Horace
never satirized an aging man's sexual desires, though that was
much more a convention of Roman comic writing than the
old(er) woman and hers. The puzzling persistence of the Old-
Woman-as-Lecher in Horace's later poetry seems the result of a
fuzzy place in Horace's own human affections that only resolved itself as he grew older: perhaps only in the last book of

odes, written around age fifty, do we find something like an admission that the poet's own desires are now as futile as hers. The epodes on this subject are wonderfully disturbing to the standard image of the "Horatian" poem as the peaceful and civilized poem of detachment. The two more realistic ones, epodes 8 and 12, speak in the character of a young stud or gigolo, the midnight cowboy of a rich, decadent circle fascinated with his sexual prowess. In both poems he is supposed to have become too disgusted with his anonymous, decrepit female client to function. Epodes 5 and 17 are Canidia poems, mimes. In the first, the old woman appears in the fantasy-guise of a mad witch brewing unthinkable love potions to satisfy her rampant lust; in the second, she threatens to destroy Horace with her magic for having exposed her to the public. In epode 5 an unlucky boy, son of respectable Roman citizens, but kidnapped for weird midnight rituals and stripped naked of his toga and bulla, begs Canidia for mercy. But she, Sagana, and other witches are determined to bury him to the head alive and starve him, in order to cut out, dry, and powder his hunger-tortured vitals for a love potion. This, she claims, will bring the faithless Varus back to her:

"You will return, Varus, nor will mere Marsian chants
enchain your mind and bring you back;
I shall prepare a greater charm, shall pour for you
in your disdain a stronger wine.
Yes, and the sky will fall and sink into the sea,
collapse and spread over the earth,
before you fail to flame with passionate love for me,
like a black blaze of bitumen!"   [*Epodes* 5.75–82]

At this the boy breaks out into imprecations, then prophesies Canidia's death at the hands of a mob when the outrage is discovered, and her being cast out, unburied, on the rubbish dump that was on the Esquiline before Maecenas built there. A sequel to this poem, epode 17, concludes the book. Horace "repents" of his exposure of Canidia, as the poet Stesichorus in archaic Greece had repented before the divine Helen who blinded him for criticizing her role at Troy. Quoting a similar poem written by Catullus thirty years before, he sarcastically offers to

call Canidia *pudica et proba*, chaste and honest. He will also call
her supposititious son "Pactumeius" (whose parentage the sac-
rificial boy had ventured to doubt in epode 5) legitimate, if she
will but spare him. Her response is negative:

> "I who can make the waxen image move and live,
> as you yourself know, prying one, and from the pole
> can tear the moon down if I like with magic chants,
> I who can resurrect the ashes of the dead,
> and brew the winecups into philtres of desire,
> shall I whine that my magic arts can't finish *you*?"
>
> [*Epodes* 17.76–81]

A fine trick, to make this last line finish not just Horace, but
the poem and also the book. (The Latin also hisses with rage:
plorem artis in te nil agentis exitus?) If Canidia is meant to be (as
commentators ancient and modern have not unnaturally suggested) a fantasy version of the more realistic old woman in
epodes 8 and 12, it is fair that she gets the last word in this
spectacular style.

For the horrible Old Woman of the *Epodes* is the most baroque and extravagant gesture in all Horace. The midnight cowboy who is the speaker in epode 8, accused of impotence, describes to the old woman her black teeth, her wrinkle-plowed
forehead, her yawning cunt like an incontinent cow's, her
mare's tits and arthritic wobbling ankles (among other details),
and asks if she expects her noble birth and pearls, and the
learned scrolls spread among her pillows that represent her as a
docta puella, an intellectual girl like Propertius's or Catullus's, to
excite him sexually. Then he compels her to fellatio in two terrific verses which, appallingly, compel the reader's mouth open
also (for the ancients did not read silently):

> quod ut superbo provoces ab inguine,
> ore allaborandum est tibi.
>
> To get response from down below such noble thighs
> hard labor waits your oral hole!   [*Epodes* 8.19–20]

Similar abuse in epode 12. "What do you want of me, woman fit only for black elephants?" Horace begins, satirizing the
old woman's main sexual preoccupation, namely, with the size

of erections. The old woman's body odor and her sweats in heat, melting the dried crocodile dung of her white face paint till it runs, are described to her in horrid detail, as the gigolo of epode 8 abuses her yet again in a different meter. None of this need be literal: if the old woman was a real person, she may not even have been that old. The language of Roman scurrility and invective is never bound by mere facts, and even as a pure creation of poetry she sounds as if she might have been no older than forty. If Horace won the favors of some wealthy patroness after Philippi, found she was more interested in his sexual than his literary abilities, and dropped her when he met Maecenas— but the language of Roman scurrility is never limited by facts.

The suite of four "Old Woman" poems, epodes 5, 8, 12, 17, is paralleled, without much regard on Horace's part for the superior dignity of Roman politics, by a suite of four Roman political poems, 1, 7, 9, 16. The opening poem offering to accompany Maecenas to Actium is paralleled by 9, placed with elaborate ingenuity half-way through the book (it starts at line 311 of the book's 625). This is a vivid, dramatic description of reactions on shipboard, seasickness included, to the battle of Actium itself: first terror, then messages of hope, then wine to kill seasickness, and triumphant cheers for Octavian. The battle is correctly described as a confused, quickly won rout, instead of the great triumph against odds it became in later Augustan propaganda, and that seems to imply that Horace fulfilled his promise in epode 1 and was there. Epodes 7 and 16 both date from earlier in the 30s, despairing poetic harangues to an imaginary assembly of Romans on the horrors of civil war that seemed at that time likely never to end. Epode 7 invokes what perhaps had just become a theme for poets and prose writers—the ancient legend of the murder of Remus by Romulus as symbol of a curse of fratricidal war that the Republic cannot shake off. Why was so much Roman blood spilled, not to conquer Carthage or Britain, but to fulfill the prayers of the Parthians and unpeople the city?

> Was this blind fury, or some more compelling cause,
> some ancient guilt? Oh, answer me!
> They are silent, deadly pallor overspreads their faces,
> their minds perplexed and thunderstruck;
> it is true. A bitter fate drives Romans on

to brothers' murder, primal curse,
since undeserving Remus shed, upon our hills,
the blood his grandsons must atone.   [*Epodes* 7.13–20]

Epode 16 asks Romans to consider whether the Golden Age
of early Italy could not be recovered by a fantastic gesture made
by all true Romans together. They should abandon the blood-
cursed site of Rome and sail off together to the Happy Isles
beyond Gibraltar, where surely war will cease and storms and
sickness be unknown. Why did Horace revive these poems in 30
B.C.? Why did he put them in this order in the book of epodes,
so that the despairing lectures on civil war (epodes 7 and 16)
alternate with the Actium epodes (1 and 9), and the second of
them comes next to last in the book, just before the second
Canidia fantasy?

When the *Epodes* were published, and Octavian had not yet
returned to Rome from Alexandria, Horace seems to have expected (and perhaps Romans in general did) something nearer a
Pompey, an authoritative first citizen of a more orderly Republic, than a Caesar, a perpetual dictator and monarch. In the
context of such an expectation, republishing these poems would
have made sense. This new leader of a Republic that had been
kept in disorder for thirty years by civil war need not be assisted
by conventional praise. Equally effective in his support would
be a warning reminder of earlier chaos, still perfectly ready to
return. Actium was not an end but a precarious beginning.

In a comic vein, the last epode, placed next to epode 16 to
conclude the book, suggests that, if we stay at Rome rather than
flee to the blessed isles, there is no salvation from the bloodshed, lust, and witchcraft Canidia symbolizes. So the joke on
which the book ends is, in context, mildly ominous, too. A
fantasy solution to our difficulties is suggested in 16: we can flee
to the Canaries and try to find the Golden Age once more,
leaving Rome deserted and ruined. Or (line 17) we *can* brave it
out in a corrupt Rome, but unless great things happen soon,
innocent boys in boys' togas and innocent and pure-minded
poets will dissolve in the garlicky flames of Canidia's dragon-
breath and the *Macbeth*-like brew of her love potions. Horace

was not encouraged, later, to be so flippant about the need for moral regeneration under a new regime.

There are also three fine epodes about love, or rather about multiple love affairs, in which Horace laments without much sincerity his own and his lovers' youthful inconstancy. Epode 15 in particular, which warns "Neaera's" new lover that however rich, however learned and intelligent, he will not be able to keep her either (*ast ego vicissim risero*," but I will laugh in my turn"), is an unintentional prophecy of the later lyric of smiling resignation to the loss of lovers, of which Horace, when older, became a master. In epode 14 he apologizes to Maecenas for the slow production of his epodes—a hint, in Callimachus's manner, that they were written with great care and scholarship—giving love-distraction as an excuse.

Epode 11, with its self-referential wit ("I write this poem because I'm too much in love to write poems") and its untrammeled poetic bisexuality, is the most brilliant of the three. It is the perfect portrait of the young, unrepentant Horace, as much the poet of the wild, promiscuous singles life as Catullus was of the ardent and passionate love affair. The decorum of the form, mathematical and precise, contrasts with the breathless violence of the content. Ten lines before and after frame Horace's account of his oration to Pettius after a wine party:

> Pettius, there's no joy for me (there was before)
> in writing couplets, struck once more with serious
>   love,
> love that hunts me down beyond all other men
> to set me aflame for girls and girlish boys again.
> Now a third winter shakes the glory from the trees
> since I forgot my passion for Inachia,
> and what a story that has made me all through Rome!
> The disgrace offends me, and the drinking parties
>   (shame)
> at which my languor and my stupid silence showed
> the lover, the long sighs I drew from deep inside.
> "Oh! Are my poet's poverty and candid mind
> worth nothing against his *money?*" I complained to
>   you,

my face on fire, when Bacchus, god of loosened
     mouths,
drew in my cups my secrets from their hiding place.
"If, in my Roman heart, a free man's rage lives on,
I should dismiss these useless treatments for a wound
to the wind; they're healing nothing. I have lost my
     shame,
or I wouldn't struggle on against such hopeless
     odds."
When my severe oration to my public—you—was
     through,
you said, "Go home." But I went home on tipsy feet
by those unfriendly doorposts—oh! and thresholds—
     oh!
and stopped again and sprawled till back and sides
     were numb.
And now Lyciscus's wolfish love, who glories so
in a soft elegance beyond kept women's dreams,
enchains me, nor can any friend's free-spoken words
loosen the snare, nor grave contempt; nothing like
     that,
but I must find another still: a fresh-faced girl,
a silky boy who ties and loosens long loose hair.
                                          [*Epodes* 11]

The sensuality of the last line of this little comedy is fierce:
aut teretis pueri longam renodantis comam, "or a smooth-skinned
boy reknotting/unknotting his long hair," where the participle
renodantis is deliberately ambiguous, as though one were meant
to see the simple action several ways: unknotting his long hair,
and untying Lyciscus's "snare" from Horace (Lyciscus is Greek
for "little wolf," but he, like the new boy, is also a setter of
traps); knotting up his long hair and snaring Horace with it, yet
again.
    This is the young Horace, the Horace not just before Au-
gustus but before "Horace," and a fine note on which to leave
him. His next publication was the *Odes* of 23 B.C., when he was
forty-two. The same themes in a grander mode are still there.
But new themes have entered Horace's poetry. Augustus, the

gods, and the empire have appeared on the scene. Horace's age has brought with it the ever-more-present thought of death and transience, and a certain tendency (at least compared to the early poems) to portray himself *en buste*, perhaps not a bad idea in middle age. Horace is never so graphic and not often so brightly passionate again in his love poetry after the early period. His later poetry explores, stage by stage, his own aging and the transformation of his society, with ever-deepening suggestions of struggle and tension and sadness. But it always looks back to the brightness of the early poetry as a model, and never fails to draw from its positive spirit the inspiration for new energy and new triumphs over challenge.

III THE CONQUEST OF A NEW GENRE

IN OR AROUND THE SUMMER OF 23 B.C., THE NINTH YEAR AFTER Augustus defeated Antony and Cleopatra at Actium, Horace published the work that is the centerpiece and crown of his whole achievement, the three books of *Odes* or *Carmina.* Starting probably in the second half of the thirties, he produced eighty-eight lyric poems, of which the longest contains eighty lines and the shortest eight. For publication they were obviously arranged in order with endless care and imagination to give them extra point to any reader who had time to consider each book individually and the three books together as a whole. The 2,456 lines of the three books (876 plus 572 plus 1,008) would represent about eight years of work at the rate of a line a day; and the achievement, the most profoundly finished, variegated, and learned book in the whole of Roman poetry, certainly justifies the time Horace spent. Not even such tireless men as Augustus and Agrippa worked harder to build monuments for themselves and for Rome.

The *Satires* had modernized Lucilius, and the *Epodes* had introduced into Latin the manner and meter of Archilochus and Hipponax. The *Odes* explicitly advertise themselves throughout as bringing into Latin the style, manner, and meter of early Greek lyric. Alcaeus and Sappho are principal models, Pindar and Bacchylides next, and after them the whole range of Greek and Latin verse from epic and drama to epigram.

Of the thirteen Greek lyric meters Horace adapted into Latin for this work, he shows off nine different ones in the first nine odes of the first book, the so-called Parade Odes. We have earlier experiments (by Catullus) in two of them only, the Sapphic and the fifth Asclepiad. Most were new to Latin. Most were never attempted again by any major Latin poet after Horace, except as professed Horatian pastiche. Examples are scarce even at that, like the one set of Alcaics and one set of Sapphics that the poet Statius inserted in his *Silvae* (ca. 90 A.D.). What Horace hoped would be a model was instead too perfect; it defied imitation.

The Greek meters are applied to a vocabulary as different as possible from that of the Greek poets Horace imitates, a purposely limited and purist vocabulary almost without compound adjectives, Greek words, or dialect and popular Latin usages. But the tone can always be brought down a little with terms from the world of business, law, the army, or just plain and direct words from standard Latin prose. There are few newly coined words. It was a convention for Latin poets to enrich their language with mildly novel words and usages in each new publication, but in the *Odes* Horace uses only about thirty-five—or less if, as is probable, he had an earlier lost authority for some of them. Nearly all such usages are (as Horace says in *The Art of Poetry* when discussing rules for coinages) *parce detorta*, "only slightly twisted," from the normal (for example, *enaviganda*, "to be sailed to the end," for *naviganda*, "to be sailed"). *Recantare*, "to recant," which translates the Greek *palinodein*, "to sing a palinode," is the only one of Horace's coinages to descend all the way down to English as a common word.

Otherwise, Horace deals in a Latin vocabulary that is very restricted, even commonplace. It is significant that of all Latin writers he is the most sparing with superlatives, as if the suffix *-issimus* was sufficient in itself to make a thought overstated and vulgar. One wonders if even Horace noticed quite how often he goes in the other direction instead by using such litotes as *non indecoro pulvere sordidus*, "dirtied with not inglorious dust." But this simple vocabulary is made poetic by elaborate juxtapositions and interlockings, so that successive words color and illuminate one another like pieces of a mosaic; in Nietzsche's deservedly famous judgment, a "mosaic of words, in which every word, by sound, by placing, and by meaning, spreads its influence to the right, to the left, and over the whole; this minimum in extent and number of symbols, this maximum thereby achieved in the effectiveness of the symbols—all this is Roman, and believe me, elegant par excellence."

In achieving this effect Horace had to satisfy the requirements of the elaborate Greek meters (which ran against the grain of the heavier sonorities of Latin), working within a restricted repertoire of words and thoughts. On the latter level he mostly confines himself to treating commonplaces of topic and theme by combining them in surprising new ways to create surprising new effects. Certainly, many phrases express some kind of paraphrasable content that had never been put in quite that way before, but they are lost among the hundreds of new ways to say old things.

Every poem in the *Odes* is thus some kind of trophy of struggle, and Horace tells the reader so several times over. Some of the finest odes are devoted in part or completely to delighted praise of Horace's own success. From the very first poem one can tell that something has happened to Horace since the *Epodes*. In the first line he invokes Maecenas, his "tower of defense and happy glory," to be his guardian genius. Another man, Horace claims, may be raised to equality with the gods on clouds of dust, the platforms of treacherous chariots, and the palms of Olympic victories. Another may achieve the consulship by winning the fickle favor of the people, while another may fill his great storehouses with all the grain of rich Africa. One man would not stir from his small farm for a kingly fortune to risk his life on the seas; another, who is a merchant and loves sea adventure, could never retire to the quiet of a farm. Some love drinking wine and wasting time by quiet fountains; some love warfare, hated by soldiers' mothers; some love hunting, forgetful of their wives, and are equally happy whether a deer or a wild boar breaks through the net. Horace, however, is committed to the poet's career.

> Thy ivy that covers the brow of true poets
> raises me to heaven; the shady sacred grove
> and the linked nymphs and choruses of satyrs
> seclude me from common men, if Euterpe plays
> the flute and Polyhymnia does not refuse
> to touch the strings of Sappho's Lesbian lyre.
> Maecenas, if you place me among the lyric poets,
> I will smite the stars with my uplifted forehead.
>
> [*Odes* 1.1.29–36]

The train of thought here is much more dense and suggestive than in the *Epodes*. Every one of Horace's examples is a challenge to consider, not only why this or that life is different from the poet's calling, but also how it resembles that calling: through vision and understanding, he suggests, the poet has all the others' riches and glories without their faults. The prologue thus offers a foretaste of the challenging originality with which he will combine familiar notions throughout the *Odes* into new and striking ensembles. The first and last examples, the charioteer and poet, are Greek, while those in between are Roman, just as Horace will blend Greek and Roman themes. But all the examples are relevant to the *poet*. The poet, too, wins dusty and difficult but famous victories, like those at the games, but his are eternal. He submits his lifework to the people's judgment, just as the consul does. He gathers the treasures of worldwide learning without generating envy and strife with his wealth. He goes daringly overseas for material without the selfish acquisitiveness of the merchant; loves elegant, contemplative leisure by the fountains of poetry, without in any sense wasting his time; describes warfare but gives no wounds; and hunts down "real toads" to put in his "imaginary gardens," whether gentle deer or mad wild boars turn up in his net.

The touch at the end of the first ode (*inseres*, "insert/ class/shelve [me]") is characteristic of the perpetual irony and self-consciousness which Horace had to display to make lyric poetry credible to his audience. Lyric poetry in this late and urbane world was like verse drama in our time. The poet had to signal to the Roman reader that he was not creating museum pieces, historic reproductions of the style of five hundred years earlier in Greece, but applying this style to the contemporary world. Thus, instead of merely saying to Maecenas, "If you consider me a lyric poet, I will be exalted to the stars," Horace says, "If you place me [that is, after you have heard all the poems] among the lyric poets" in your library of scrolls. This is to be a modern Roman book, aspiring to its proper classification (what we would call its catalogue number) in Rome's private and public libraries.

Ode 2.20, the tailpiece of the second book, is a similar example of the innovation and daring without which Horace knew that lyric poetry would not work in his time. Horace not only claims to have built his own monument during his lifetime (as many Romans did) and made extravagant mourning at his funeral unnecessary. He already feels—knows—that his poetry will be read forever throughout Augustus's empire, even in provinces like Dacia (Rumania), whose conquest was still only projected in 23 B.C.

> On unaccustomed wings, but broad and strong,
> through liquid aether, bird and poet
> soon shall I fly. Not here on earth
> shall I stay quiet, but above your carping
> shall leave your cities. I am the poor blood
> of humble parents, merely the friend
> whom you ask over, dear Maecenas.
> But the dark Styx will not constrain me;
> I shall not die. Now on my legs the harsh
> skin folds and blackens; my upper body
> becomes a swan; on my fingers
> and shoulders delicate feathers sprouting
> show that, renowned farther than Icarus,
> I shall look down on the Black Sea's wailing shore,
> on Sidra's gulf, Morocco; singing
> musically to the Arctic northlands.
> Children of Colchis, Dacians who sham defiance
> of south Italian cohorts, and the farthest
> Ukrainians will know me. Clever Spaniards
> and men who drink the Rhone will learn me
> by heart. Around my cenotaph moaning
> chants are in vain, complaint's disgraceful.
> Cut short your clamor, spare my
> empty sarcophagus its honors.   [*Odes* 2.20]

Horace could not have made himself just another Pindaric swan of the generic brand. Without some kind of added realism and irony, that would have come off as mere poetic furniture. Instead he describes in detail a stranger bird, a guest of Maecenas's, with skin suddenly blackening on his legs and (in a metaphor borrowed from Plato's *Phaedrus*) the feathers of his soul sprouting, one by one. Horace intentionally mocks the idea of metamorphosis with his realistic description of the black skin, the first thing visible from below to the astonished Maecenas as he sails off. He needs both realism and humor to carry off any such statement about himself to his Roman audience.

When Horace pictured himself soaring above Maecenas's townhouse and looking down, from the dizzying heights of immortality, on the map of the empire and the rest of the known world of 23 B.C., he was alluding to real maps that were found in his and his friends' libraries. In Rome, map making and geography had long been high-priority items supported by government-paid research. It was one of Agrippa's long-term projects to set up as a public monument a colossal map of the known world. Incorporating the latest geographical research, and annotated with distances and descriptions of cities, the map would be of practical use to the Roman people at a time when prose writers and poets, Horace included, were praising the growing facility of travel as one of the great boons of the imperial peace. (The monument was not finished and dedicated until the year of Horace's death.)

Thus Horace, like that very different sort of self-celebrator, Whitman, made his speech "the twin of his vision" in the *Odes*. His image of the swan is familiar from Greek poetry, but drastically modernized; his invocation of Maecenas and allusion to the map are drawn from contemporary Roman life. Horace's descriptions of these familiar themes, and the ensemble they make, are as new and audacious as his poetic technique and style.

Personality and audaciousness, not just technique and style, inform every line of the *Odes*. They are not loved for that "gentle Horatian wisdom" the Victorians professed to find in them, but because they have taught so many generations of readers, as no other poetry can so effectively teach, what poetry *is*. The perfect fit of words and meanings with recurrent strophic meter; the perpetual challenge in every apparently simple word to consider why it is the right word for right here; the endless forcing of the reader to stop and ask, Why this list of names? Why this change of thought? Why this sudden intrusion of something grand into a very simple passage, or vice versa?—all these demand reflection at every line. The *Odes* are short poems.

Even a not unusually sensitive or "literary" reader can see from
end to end of them and come up with answers to these questions that work in a surprising number of cases. As for the
poems' verse-music, Horace has taught millions what the music
of words can be. Izaak Walton tells us that a seventeenth-
century Anglican bishop, Dr. Sanderson, who knew the *Odes* by
heart, said that "the repetition of one of the Odes of Horace was
to him such music, as a lesson on the viol was to others, when
they played it to themselves or friends." Similar compliments
have been paid to the *Odes* in every age, whatever its judgment
of Horace's message.

It would be a shame even in a short treatment of the *Odes* to
leave out any illustration of Horace's metrical technique. Latin
verse can be read satisfactorily (if roughly) out loud by treating
the ictus or verse accent, in reality produced by long and short
syllables, as a mere word accent; but the best way is, of course,
to read the syllables as long and short.* In the following eight-
line love poem, the Latin is marked with verse accents and the
syllables with their proper quantities. The line-by-line literal
translation is intended only to make the Latin clear. I hope that
the sound and rhythm of the short poem will reveal something
about Horace that would not be clear from a simple exposition of
the meaning and structure of the *Odes*.

In the eighty-eight odes the commonest meters are Alcaic
(thirty-three odes) and Sapphic (twenty-three).

Alcaic	Sapphic
‒‿‒‒‒‿‿‒‿‒	‒‿‒‒‒‿‿‒‿‒‒
‒‿‒‒‒‿‿‒‿‒	‒‿‒‒‒‿‿‒‿‒‒
‒‿‒‒‒‿‒‿‒	‒‿‒‒‒‿‿‒‿‒‒
‒‿‿‒‿‿‒‿‒‒	‒‿‿‒‒

These four-line stanzas are described in every handbook of
poetry, and James Michie's translation of the *Odes*, recommended in my bibliographical note, contains a number of bril-

---

*Except that *c*'s and *g*'s are always hard, and that *ae* should be pronounced
like long *i* ("I") in English, Latin can be read with the same consonants as in
English and the same vowels as Spanish or Italian to get the approximate effect.
V's were still pronounced about like our *w*'s in Horace's day and for a few
generations after, but that is not as crucial in reading aloud.

liant experiments in rendering these two meters into English. Tennyson's "Milton: Alcaics" is the most perfect antiquarian representation of the effect of this Latin meter in English.

> Where some refulgent sunset of India
> Streams o'er a rich ambrosial ocean isle,
> And crimson-hued and stately palmwoods
> Whisper in odorous heights of even.

One could transform this (not so well as Tennyson could have) into an English Sapphic as:

> Some refulgent sunset above the Indies,
> O'er a rich ambrosial ocean islet,
> Where the windblown boughs of the stately
> palmwoods
> Whisper at even.

My own translations from these meters, though they fall into four-line stanzas, aim only at a sort of impressionistic, free-form representation. All but five of the remaining thirty-two odes are in various forms of the Asclepiadic line, built by beginning with a spondee ($--$), then adding either one, two, or three choriambs ($-\smile\smile-$), followed by an iamb ($\smile-$) or a single syllable. To make this clearer, I have separated by a space the syllables that form the choriambs, even when that means breaking up words with a slash. Ode 1.11 illustrates the longest of these lines, the greater asclepiad ($--$ $-\smile\smile-$ $-\smile\smile-$ $-\smile\smile-$ $\smile-$).

> tú ne quaésierís (scíre nefás) quém mihi, quém tibí
> fínem dí dederínt, Leúconoé, néc Babylón / iós
> témptar / ís numerós. út meliús quídquid erít patí,
> seú plur / ís hiemés seú tribuít Iúppiter úl / timám
> quáe nunc óppositís débilitát púmicibús maré
> Túrrhen / úm: sapiás, vína liqués, ét spatió breví
> spém long / ám resecés. dúm loquimúr, fúgerit ín / vidá
> aétas; cárpe diém, quám minimúm crédula pós / teró.

> You should not inquire (it is wrong to know) what
>   fate to me, to you
> the gods may have given, Leuconoe, nor should you

> try the Babylonian
> horoscopes. How much better to suffer whatever shall
>   be,
> whether Juppiter offers more winters or [only this, as
>   the] last,
> which now is shattering, on the porous rocks that
>   oppose it,
> the Etruscan sea. Show better taste [or: Be sensible],
>   strain the wine, and from our brief life
> trim the long hopes. While we are talking, envious
>   Time
> will have fled: pluck the day, trusting as little as
>   possible to the next.

Anyone can see by looking at the Latin what a tour de force this poem is. The language is as simple as always. There are only four "epithets"; and only one is unusual—the pompous and mocking "Babylonian" for the horoscopes. "Short" life and "long" hopes are made interesting by the metaphor of "trimming" them back" (like vines) and the sharp antithetical contrast in which they stand, "envious" Time by the tense of the verb ("will have fled," already, irrevocably). The middle choriamb of the three must always be separated by a caesura, or break, before and after the other words. Only eight of the twenty-four choriambs required by the eight lines run across words; but no two successive lines use the same pattern of separation and run-on. The secret of this kind of metrical tour de force in Latin lyric dies with Horace; his few imitators could produce only the palest shadow of his mastery.

The Odes in Their Roman Context: Lovers

If we turn from the meter and style of Odes 1.11 to its content, this short love poem is as original as the two poems about poetry quoted earlier. It belongs to no one genre classification (drinking-poem, advice-poem, love-poem) at all, though it borrows from the conventions of several. Horace is arguing on a winter evening with a girlfriend that it doesn't matter if his horoscope is incompatible with hers; why even inquire? "Scire *nefas"*: it is not just wrong but violates the divine law to know. That should be our rule, too, whether astrology is real or not. Why find out if the winter outside that breaks the sea on the pumicelike volcanic rocks is the last? The destruction of the waves and the wearing down of the rock both become symbols of the fragility of life and the chaos of nature. The consonants in lines 3–6 are all arranged to suggest the pounding and violence of the storm. Their meaningless chaos is the flat refutation of hopeful efforts like astrology to impose meaning on the chaos of human fate.

Astrology was not yet the universal terror it became in the hag-ridden times of the late empire, but Augustus (moon in Capricorn) and his successors consulted astrologers as a matter of course. Maecenas probably believed in them. Horace in a later poem (*Odes* 2.17) consents to compare horoscopes with him while trying to console his patron in one of the fits of hypochondria and fear of death from which Maecenas frequently suffered (as we know from other sources). This poem, too, has the air of depicting a particular situation in real life. Leuconoe, "white [simple, sincere] mind," is barely attested as a personal name in Greek and must be a nickname. It is "white-minded" and good-hearted of her to believe in such magic.

But that accords with her being simple and housewifely around her (Horace's?) table. She strains the wine, which you only did to drink it right *now*, for sediment could be left to settle if there was time. "Trimming" long hopes as if they were vines to fit a short life, and "plucking" the day like an apple in an orchard, belong to the same pattern. Horace unobtrusively makes clear that astrology is not just wrong but morally wrong (*nefas*), even if it worked, and that Leuconoe is credulous (*credula*). But he downplays his conviction that astrology is a fraud, as if stating his own Epicurean beliefs more strongly would be unaffectionate and patronizing. Horace's concern is to present the real reason to love and seize the day: that life is too unpredictable and violent, like the winter storm.

Such details build a characterization of Leuconoe that Horace cannot be supposed to have drawn from earlier literature. Like other poets, he wrote and published this sort of poem "about" real people and "from" real experiences, though of course without making himself remotely responsible for the factuality of every detail, and combining impressions from several experiences rather than one. For all the learning and technique he applies to writing verse, Horace's poems to lovers are reflections of unique situations, not mere poetic conventionalities.

Similarly, the Rome Horace pictures is not a mere literary construct, but a real and exciting city. The Greeks who attend his parties and make up the roll of his lovers really lived there; they were as familiar at the entertainments of the political dignitaries and friends to whom odes are addressed as they were at Horace's own.* If Greek demimondaines and fancy boys, intelligent, literary and amusing, turn up at Horace's parties and picnics, that is not because Horace is mechanically mixing Roman details with imaginary Greek ones, but because Augustan Rome, its palaces, its suburban gardens, its country towns and villas were full of such people, many of them with the very names—Chloe, Galatea, Myrtale, Tyndaris, Lycidas—Horace gives them.

Moreover, as was natural since the political and financial interests of Greece had been dominated by Rome for 150 years, thousands of free Greek provincials chose to live in Rome for profit and excitement. Antony had hoped to defeat Augustus by appropriating the East to himself: when Augustus's regime began, the Greek-speaking part of the empire was not only half of it but by far the more advanced and prosperous half. There were independent businesswomen named Lydia in Rome as well as in St. Paul's Thyatira; one doesn't need to look to early Greek poets' Lydias to find "models" for Horace's. And again, these people's manners were still less bound by Roman convention than those of the imperial Greek slaves and freedpersons. Those who were out for amusement had no objection to associating with Italians. As the poet and philosopher Philodemus of Gadara, an acquaintance of Cicero's, Vergil's, and most probably the young Horace's, says of one of his Italian girlfriends:

---

*In what follows I am indebted to Jasper Griffin's pathbreaking essay "Augustan Poetry and the Life of Luxury," chapter 1 of his *Augustan Poetry and Roman Life* (Oxford, 1985).

> O most artistic technique in bed! O unparalleled
> kisses, and O—destroy me!—the things she says
>   there.
> What if she's Oscan, called Flora, and cannot sing
>   Sappho!
> Perseus loved Andromeda; *she* was from India.
>
> [Epigram 12.5–8]

Some of these Greeks wanted money for their favors; others sought influence, in a society that was all patronage from top to bottom. Wealthy equestrians like Horace, who had the friendship of men like Maecenas, Messalla, Pollio, and Augustus, could be as much help to their lovers as to people like the Pompey of *Odes* 2.7. Greek women like Lyde (3.17) could be invited to dinner by Horace, drink with him through sunset, and join him in duets about Diana and the Nereids, concluding with praises of Venus and the Night. As Philodemus's poem shows, it was a point against a lover of this kind not to know something about music and poetry.

Moreover, there was romance of a kind to relationships with Greeks of this class. What separates romance from finance is that the other persons choose or reject you as they please; these were people with property and servants of their own, and well above the poverty level. They were under no compulsion to come to anyone's dinners, or sing for their dinner, or stay for the night. Whatever favors they expected in return from people of Horace's station and higher could be left understood and put off till later, not demanded right away.

Moreover, as Horace says (*Epistles* 2.1.156), "Captured Greece captured her uncivilized captor, and brought the arts to rustic Latium"—and the process was still going on. Everything elegant and impressive in Rome and its environs was influenced by Greek models and architects. The masses of mythological statuary and painting in public and private houses, and parks, and gardens were executed by Greeks. They were there to suggest immediately and visibly the poetic details for treatments of the old myths of Europa, or the Danaids, or the wars of the Olympians and the Titans. The temples and squares, the baths, theaters, and libraries that Augustus and Agrippa were lavishly building from scratch or repairing and rescuing from the Republican aristocracy's selfish neglect; the great senatorial houses and the suburban villas—all were planned mostly on Greek models, many by Greek architects working with Roman engineers, and painted and decorated by more Greeks. The music and entertainments at the parties of great men and their more prosperous clients were supplied mainly by Greeks. And there were Greek poets, good ones (like Philodemus), who lived in Rome and Italy, whom Horace probably knew, and whose poetry directly influenced his. So the line of living poetic tradition in Greek was unbroken from Homer's days to Horace's own. Not even the mere technique of Horace's verse is borrowed solely from Greeks long dead.

The huge Campus Martius, grassy throughout the year, was the great Roman park, beautifully decorated even under the stingy Republic and large enough for riding and chariot racing as well as ball games, wrestling, and swimming in the Tiber. By the time Augustus had finished adorning it with yet more vast new buildings and exercise tracks and artworks, it was, as the contemporary Greek geographer and world traveler Strabo said, like a great painted stage set "from which it is hard to tear yourself away" and which seemed "to declare the rest of the city a mere appendage."

Horace had limited himself in the *Satires* to picturing himself exercising there, but the display of so much youth and prowess on the Campus had its more frivolous side. In 1.8 Lydia is reproached for keeping Sybaris (both names suggest luxuriousness) indoors for making love so continually that his admirers on the Campus no longer see him riding, swimming, wrestling, practicing arms or hurling the javelin or spear; has he become like Achilles among the maidens of Scyros, avoiding military service against Troy? The Campus in spring is where Thaliarchus can ignore the paradoxical winter storm that roars outside the wine party in *Odes* 1.9, and be teased by girls laughing provocatively in the shadows. In 3.12 Neobule ("new thoughts/rebellious") is pictured in running Ionics ($\smile\smile--$): "She is one who / must obey her / cruel uncle, / but her spinning / and her weaving / Cupid hinders / with the thought of

> Liparean Hebrus's glitter
> when he washes oily shoulders in the swift waves of
> the Tiber;
> better horseman than Bellerophon himself and never
> conquered
> in a running match or boxing . . . .

> Liparáei nitor Hébri
> simul únctos Tiberínis umerós lavit in úndis,
> eques ípso meliór Bellerophónte, neque púgno
> neque ségni pede víctus . . . .   [*Odes* 3.12.6–9]

"Liparean Hebrus": the Greek roots suggest brightness, (wrestling) oil, and a Thracian river, so the Greek boy from Lipara is already, by virtue of his name and place, the Oiled/ Shiny Swimmer. Even Greek girls of respectable family can wander about the Campus in the afternoon and admire the athletes from a distance. At the end of *Odes* 4.1 Horace dreams of the unattainable boy Ligurinus, for once an Italian name:

> In my dreams at night I now hold you
> wrestled and won, now follow you racing
> through the grassy Campus Martius,
> or down the flowing—harsh one!—waters.

> [*Odes* 4.1.37–40]

In 2.5, Horace pictures his rueful forty-year-old self looking round a crowd of beautiful younger people, and, as the second stanza makes obvious by its metaphors, in exactly this setting:

> Her neck cannot bend under and take the yoke,
> she cannot respond to a yokemate's energy;
> she cannot take the weight of a bull
> that charges into love in heat.
> Your heifer's mind is all round
> the grassy fields [*campi*], now in the water
> solacing heavy heat, now longing
> to play with the young calves
> in the wet reeds. Away with this lust
> for the unripe grape; soon Autumn

with his many hues will paint
the green clusters purple.
Soon she will follow you; speedily Time
in her account will place as credits
the years you lose; with eager face
Lalage will pursue her husband,
delightful as teasing Pholoe never was,
nor Chloris, shining with white shoulder
as the unclouded moon shines back to
the night sea, as Cnidian Gyges shines,
who, if enrolled in a chorus of girls,
would wondrously trick even clever strangers,
a puzzling judgment, with his loose
long hair and his ambiguous face.   [*Odes* 2.5]

As this poem opens Horace is lost in what for the *Odes* are
unusually explicit thoughts of what Lalage might be like in bed
if she were not so young. For once he seems to think of the
woman as a wife: *iugum* (yoke) and *munia* (marital duties) are
both words that are used of animals, but suggest marriage
rather than love affairs when used of people. He makes her
sound, not like a "mere" Greek, but independent, energetic,
and attractively indifferent to what others, including Horace,
may be thinking about her.

But that brings the thought of passing time. In financial
language, the years that Time will "put to her account" will be
"withdrawals" from Horace's own: age will make her more attractive and himself less. Apparently it is because of this dis-
couraging thought that his eye meditatively drifts round the
circle of the fashionable young on the Campus, stopping on one
and another, and comes to rest on Gyges: for the principal attraction of involvements with boys, the ancients thought, was
that they were briefer and less serious than those with women.
So the uncomfortable thought of time is exorcised with a linger-
ing glance at Gyges' girlish face and (regulation) long hair.
Every line of the poem redoes some suggestion from Anacreon,
Alcaeus, Sappho, Philodemus. But Horace has brought his originals into a juxtaposition all his own, and into a fresh new sce-

nery where even Greeks like Strabo, who had seen the ancient glories of Greece in detail, were dazzled.

The background of all the love poems (as in the *Epodes*) is that of a real and literally "fast" world of singles that existed only in Rome and a few aristocratic resort towns like Tibur and Baiae. Allegiances change quickly. The simple-appearing but stormy-tempered Pyrrha of ode 1.5 is someone else's now and he may have her, "for the votive tablet on the sacred wall shows I have hung up my wet garments to the sea-god" (by which Horace means Neptune and Venus at once). But Horace has been through the full sea storm, even if he only ended up where he started: unloved again.

Lydia can be reproached with the marks that Telephus's violent lovemaking have left on her shoulders and lips, for Horace had hoped for more faith: "Happy are they three times and more whose bonds are never broken, whose love is destroyed by no evil quarrels and lets them go only on the deathday" (*Odes* 1.13.17–20). With grave, sudden authority Horace reveals that he knows perfectly what sort of love he will never find among such companions, love of which life and death themselves are the measure. But this is seldom Horace's note. More typical is an extraordinary juxtaposition early in book 3. The crown of Horace's state poetry, the set of Roman Odes (3.1–6), has just come to its pompous moralistic conclusion when Horace rallies poor Asterie in 3.7. He knows Gyges is faithful to her, although her lover has been stranded on his way back from Bithynia with his merchandise and besieged by his host's amorous wife. So she must not, Horace tells her, be attracted by Enipeus as, once more, he exercises on the Campus or swims in the Tiber.

It is true that Horace's portrait of this world and of himself in it is sometimes a little distasteful, not at all for its frankness, but for occasional hints of obsessions that have not been fully and convincingly made into poetry. All the splendid rhetoric and realism he puts into the two rather gratuitous poems to the repulsive but oversexed old women of the *Odes* (in 1.25, for instance, which prophesies frustration for the suddenly aging Lydia, or 3.15, which predicates it of Chloris) leaves these poems rather sterile compared to epodes 8 and 12.

> Rarer and rarer on the shuttered window
> Their taps' insistence, nor do your avid friends
> Keep you from dreaming now that the same door is
>   Hugging the doorpost
> That had such practice swinging wide and open
> On easy hinges.
>
> [*Odes* 1.25.1–6; Andras Hamori translation]

As an old woman Lydia will be only a scarecrow among the circle of young Greeks who reject her. In that respect she seems a projection of the poet's own fears of becoming involved with people his own age and of being rejected by the young. Horace takes a significantly kinder tone toward himself when he speaks as a man of the same age, whose siege of a young woman's doors is unsuccessful:

> My life as a man for girls is over,
> though my soldiering won much glory:
> now all my armor and that war relic,
> my lyre, shall be displayed on the wall
> that guards the left flank of Venus,
> sailor's protectress; torches of rope,
> that blazed with pitch, once; crowbars,
> siege machines for lofty doors.
> Goddess, wealthy queen of Cyprus,
> of Memphis that never saw the northern snow,
> princess of Heaven, raise your whip,
> one touch of it for arrogant Chloe!   [*Odes* 3.26]

That love is war is of course a cliché of ancient poetry, and so are dedications to Venus and the idea that the rejected lover threatens his mistress's door with burglar's tools and siege engines. But the dedication of these baroquely humorous "weapons" to the statue holding a lowered scourge has touches that are Horace's alone. He remembered everything he read, including an epithet (not particularly exciting at first glance) used by the fifth-century B.C. lyric poet Bacchylides: *acheimantòn Memphin* (fragment 30), "snowless Memphis." He also knew from Herodotus that the Greeks in Egypt called the goddess Hathor of Memphis "Foreign Aphrodite." Egyptian Venus in her mystic desert temple has never heard of such ice as is in Chloe's heart, and the statue, as in some horror story about Egyptian magic, suddenly raises its fantastic whip.

Such extravagant splendors of detail almost, but not quite, disarm the criticism that Horace is in the end no such profound or serious love poet as his contemporaries Catullus, Propertius, and Tibullus. The Old-Woman-as-Lecher, the Young Girl, the poems of pretended resignation to the coming end of Horace's career as a lover (always with a suggestion of just one more triumph to come), and much else in the love poetry of *Odes* 1–3 strike notes that are left unresolved. In later poems, especially the odes of book 4, Horace takes up some of these bachelor's themes again, and does deal with them more deeply and resolve them.

The pictures Horace draws of many of his affairs show an affection for his lovers that is as real and mature, though not much deeper, as his affection for his friends. In 1.17, "Velox amoenum saepe Lucretilem," Horace leads the reader to suppose that the poem will be a hymn to Faunus, the Roman Pan, asking the god to protect his farm. Actually, book 3 contains three hymns to the gods and spirits of the farm: 3.13 to the fountain of Bandusia, 3.18 to Faunus, and 3.22 to Diana. Faunus often leaves Arcadian Mt. Lycaeus, and comes "swiftly" to "pleasant" (the first two words) Sabine Lucretilis, keeping the summer and the rains from the goats. So the "smelly billygoat's wives" can wander (in the usual maze of interwoven Latin words) round the grove grazing on arbutus and thyme, safe from the snakes and wolves—"as often as music echoes through the valley, O Tyndaris, for the gods love my piety and my muse equally." Here is a safe place for her to avoid the summer heat and sing of "Penelope and Circe, both in trouble over the same man." But the heat, like the amorous goats and the snakes and wolves, prompts another of Horace's startling but unerring turns of thought. Tyndaris is safe with him, and with Faunus, from a violent and jealous lover in the city: "Here you will drink light Lesbian wine [a real wine, but suggesting Sappho's poems anyway as part of the concert] and Dionysus the son of Semele will mix no battle gods into the cups. You need not fear hot Cyrus's jealousy, or that he will lay violent hands on a girl who is no is no match for him, or tear the garland that sticks in your hair, or your poor undeserving clothes." Tyndaris, that is, is safe from the wolves and snakes and sadistic lovers in Rome, but not from the sensuality in which Faunus makes the farm riot, or from her own song about virtuous Penelope and magic Circe, both of whose roles Tyndaris knows how to perform.

A second poem to a fellow musician is as extravagantly sensual, and very significantly placed just before the two great odes to Maecenas (3.29) and to the book with which the whole collection ends (3.30). In 3.28, Lyde is with Horace on the Neptunalia, probably again at the Sabine farm. She also is a musician, and the ancient Caecuban wine "of the vintage of Bibulus" (who was consul in 59 B.C.)—a simpler-minded joke than most of Horace's—is to be poured freely.

> And we will sing in alternation
> of Neptune, and of the Nereids combing their sea-
> green
> hair. Your stanza for lyre and strings
> deals with Leto, and Diana's death-swift arrows:
> the last duet tells of Venus, gazing
> from her car of swans on Cnidos, Paphos,
> and the bright Cyclades, her kingdom:
> and Night too must be paid her lullaby.
>
> [*Odes* 3.28.9–16]

Horace gives the male god of the sea but one word, then turns to the Nereids, and Tyndaris follows with Venus as the goddess of the islands, and the goddess of Venus's sacred time, the Night. The poem is for the occasion and is itself the occasion—a work of art as gift to a fellow artist, as well as to a lover. So many of the love odes are gifts to a beautiful person, as the poems to patrons are gifts. The person hides irrecoverably under a symbolic name ("Lyde" suggests Lydian, soft, music) and attributes from earlier poetry. The situation lies concealed under literary allusion to earlier poets and poetic transformation and convention, and an artful refusal to pursue details of description, leaving many features of the scene uncertain. But there is always the here-and-now of real Roman and Italian scenery and social detail, and the originality of the poetic situation and ensemble, to make the feeling of a voice not purely impersonal, a situation not merely universal, inescapable in them all.

Horace's Friends: Danger, Death, and Riches

Friendship does not take such precedence over love in the lyrics as in the *Satires* and *Epodes;* but it appropriates a large place and some of the most serious themes—the universality of death, the transience of innocent pleasures, the terror and strain of Roman politics. Horace's odes to friends, about some of whom we know a good deal from other sources, seem as pointedly addressed to each in detail as those of his unknowable lovers. They too tended to be written off by the nineteenth century as strings of philosophical commonplaces with "name of patron" inserted afterwards by Horace's mental computer to gain whatever favors he needed by publishing an ode. But that (besides involving a theory of Horace's position vis-à-vis his noble friends that implies far too much humility) turns out simply not to be the case.

The lovers of the *Odes* bring the thought of death into Horace's head only once or twice. It turns up in the Leuconoe ode (1.11) as the distant winter storm, and in the Thaliarchus ode (1.9) lurking behind the image of winter/old age that generates the poem's "now." Love till death is a light romantic cliché; so is a sudden moment of seriousness about staying with one lover till death, which never happens nor can. But many of Horace's male friends had been through political danger and the risk of death in battle in the real world. Many had switched sides more than once to save themselves. (Messalla had been for Brutus, and then Antony, before he made his very profitable decision for Octavian.) All of them had survived and won riches that dwarfed Horace's own, for the various sides needed their deaths and the confiscation of their wealth less than their influence with the armies and with clients not just in Rome but around the world. It is apropos of this wealth, of expensive real estate, of splendid Roman houses and villas and gardens and picnics, that the thought of life-threatening political danger and of death always comes into the *Odes* in its full power.

Political trouble, infamy: L. Munatius Plancus, consul in 42 and censor in 22, the founder of modern Lyons, had become consul by joining the triumvirs in 43 and acquiescing in the proscription of many friends, among them his correspondent Cicero and his own half-brother Plotius Plancus, a diehard conservative. Then he had joined Antony and Cleopatra. She was rightly suspicious of him, for he deserted them and attacked Antony so violently on Octavian's behalf in the Senate that one of the senators said, "What a number of crimes Antony committed the day before you left him, Plancus!" He was now the richest magnate in Tibur, the township that embraced the Sabine farm, and Horace, who apparently believed his claim that he wasn't guilty of Plotius Plancus's death, lays out for him in ode 1.7 the glories of the Tibur that they both admire:

> Anio's fine cascade, Tiburnus' grove and the orchards
>   Whose rivulets weave a dance of irrigation.
> But the rivulets bring the thought of danger, storm
>   and the high seas with them:
> Winds from the south blow clear, they sweep clouds
>   out of a dark sky
> And never breed long rains: remember, Plancus,
> Good wine does just that for the wise man—chases
>   away all
> The stresses and distresses of existence.
> Hold to this truth in the camp, hemmed round by the
>   glittering standards,
> And, when you come home soon to Tibur's leafy
> Privacy, keep it in mind. When Teucer was sent into
>   exile
> From Salamis by his father, undismayed he
> Set on his wine-flushed brow, they say, brave
>   garlands of poplar,*
> And cried to his dispirited companions:
> "Fortune will prove more kind than a parent.
>   Wherever she takes us
> Thither, my friends and comrades, we shall follow.
> Teucer shall lead and his star shall preside. No cause
>   for despair, then.

*The symbol of Hercules.

Phoebus, who never lies, has pledged a second
Salamis, rival in name, to arise in a new-found
   country.
You who have stayed by me through worse
   disasters,
Heroes, come, drink deep, let wine extinguish our
   sorrows.
We take the huge sea on again tomorrow."
                         [*Odes* 1.7.13–32; James Michie translation]

The mythological hero Teucer had two things in common
with Plancus: he founded a city, as Plancus founded Lyons, and
he had been unjustly suspected of treachery by his implacable
father Telamon because of his half-brother Ajax's death at Troy.
Apparently daring, realistic, and close to the bone as it is in
alluding to Plancus's personal troubles, the ode succeeded with
its addressee better than more conventional panegyric would
have done.

Riches and death: Lucius Sestius was an old friend from the
days of Philippi who had been Brutus's quaestor and still kept
an image of him in his house. When the *Odes* were published in
23, Augustus, finding that his tenure of too many successive
consulships had rendered him unpopular with the nobility, had
just invented other titles and powers for himself and resigned
his consulship to Sestius as a conciliatory gesture. So Horace
shifted an ode to Sestius into fourth place after the opening
poems to Maecenas, Augustus, and Vergil:

Winter weathers away, goes dull as spring
Blows in, warm; dried-out boats
Creak to the water; sheep run from the barn;
Farmers leave their kitchen fires,
And the white, frosted meadows go brown
And green. Venus is whirling under the moon,
With all her worshippers—and Graces and Nymphs
Cross the earth on gentle feet—and burning
Vulcan comes to the Cyclops' forges.

It is time, it is time: take flowers from the new
Earth and hang them in your hair, hang myrtle

Across your forehead, and bring Faunus what he
    wants:
A lamb, a kid, and under arching trees
Offer him blood.

Death raps his boney knuckles, bleached,
Indifferent, on any man's door, a place or a hut.
Life runs short: even your money, Sestius,
Even all your money, won't buy him off.
You'll drop in his darkness, and stay forever
In shadows and mists, down in Pluto's grey hall.
No spinning the dice for toastmaster, then,
No staring, heartsick, at lovely Lycidas,
Loved by all the boys, now,
Loved by all the girls, soon.

[1.4; Burton Raffel translation]

In the original some touches appear that don't in this translation. Death kicks the doors in a wonderful series of plosives:
pállida mórs aequó pulsát pede paúperúm tabérnas. Sestius only "ad-
mires" Lycidas, as he or Horace himself might do on the Campus. All the boys are "hot" (*calent*) for Lycidas, whereas the girls
will be (as the seasons change from spring to summer) more
mildly, or less superficially, "warm" (*tepebunt*). Riches bring the
thought of death and transience into the spring.

Real estate—Roman palaces, splendid Italian villas in
splendid places—is a recurrent theme in the *Odes,* and the
thought of death and care regularly accompanies it. Augustus
wanted his rich to spend more on public buildings and less on
magnificent private palaces. Horace's way of backing up this
program is to remind great builders continually of their own
transience and the mockery their great houses make of the puny
mortal owners (*Odes* 2.14.21–28, 2.18.15–40, 3.1.25–48, 3.24.1–
8). But nothing is more prominent in his poetry than the gloom-
iness suggested by the beautiful lands and gardens and the rest
of the apparatus of luxury, whose apparent ownership-in-
perpetuity conceals our transience. The thought of death hangs
always over them.

The clever Q. Dellius had been on every side at one time or
another, and was especially remembered as one of the great wits

and intriguers of Antony and Cleopatra's court. Like Plancus he deserted them, just in time to stay alive. Another wine connoisseur, he was famous for having said discontentedly at their table as the war with Octavian drew near: "Here we are drinking vinegar while the other side drink Falernian at Rome." As the water struggles deliciously in his gardens past the embrace of the "great" pine and the "white" poplar—the symbols in Horace's "simple" language of male and female—he is advised to bring out wine (Falernian, in fact) and perfumed oil "and the too brief flowers of the scented rose":

> Be quick while the
> Dark threads the three grim Sisters weave still
> Hold and your years and the times allow it.
>
> Soon farewell town house, country estate by the
> Brown Tiber washed, chain-acres of pasture land,
> Farewell the sky-high piles of treasure
> Left with the rest for an heir's enjoyment
>
> Rich man or poor man, scion of Inachus
> Or beggar wretch lodged naked and suffering
> God's skies—it's all one. You and I are
> Victims of never-relenting Orcus,
>
> Sheep driven deathward. Sooner or later Fate's
> Urn shakes, the lot comes leaping for each of us
> And books a one-way berth in Charon's
> Boat, on the journey to endless exile.
>
> [*Odes* 2.3.14–28; James Michie translation]

Victima nil miserantis Orci: literally, "victim of Orcus who pities nothing"—a strong phrase in a society whose religion still sacrificed real victims in quantity. There was no difference not only between rich man and miserable, but between man and animal: one death unto them both. Like the rich and loyal Republican Sestius, the Epicurean Dellius, the veteran of Cleopatra's revels, may well have found this line of thought as acceptable as a more conventional poem of praise would have been. Horace finds his way to balance and equality with his addressees by any and every means, and the leveling power of death, even, is an acceptable topic in reminder.

The equally rich but religious and happily married Postumus gets a poem (*Odes* 2.14) that suggests that, like Pettius in
epode 11, he reluctantly allowed Horace a cup or two too many
of wine and made him too talkative before they looked round
his gardens and carefully kept trees.

> Alas, deserting us, Postumus, Postumus,
> the years flow past, not does piety bring delay
> to wrinkles, and menacing age,
> and unconquerable death.

The doubled name—as if Horace in mid-speech realized the
ominous implications of the surname Postumus for children
born after their fathers' deaths and repeated it with wonder—
and the double image of age and death as an indomitable tide
and army before both of which we have to retreat, are as impressive the hundredth time one reads these lines as they were
the first. There is a modern translation I like, by Basil Bunting,
as grim and bald as the seventeenth-century Pindarics of Dryden's and Congreve's translations are florid and expansive:

> You can't grip years, Postume,
> that ripple away nor hold back
> wrinkles and, soon now, age,
> nor can you tame death.
>
> not if you paid three hundred
> bulls every day that goes by
> to Pluto, who has no tears,
> who has dyked up
>
> giants where we'll go abroad,
> we who feed on the soil,
> to cross, kings some, some
> penniless plowmen.
>
> For nothing we keep out of war
> or from screaming spindrift
> or wrap ourselves against autumn,
> for nothing, seeing
>
> we must stare at that dark, slow
> drift and watch the damned

toil while all they build
tumbles back on them.

We must let earth go and home,
wives too, and your trim trees,
yours for a moment, save one
sprig of black cypress.

Better men than we will empty
bottles we locked away,
wine puddle our table,
fit wine for a pope.

Tinguet pavimentum [mero] superbo / pontificum potiore cenis
("[Your heir] will stain the marble pavement with wine better
than the high priests' dinners"): the wine held back in the third
line spills dactylically in the fourth in a rain of drunken p's, t's,
and c's.

Once more, "we" are the equal voyagers to death, equally
cautious of sea, war, and illness—the sirocco and the dreaded
Roman fever that could kill thousands in a single autumn. Both
Horace and Postumus were in a position to leave for the country
and avoid it. But it is Postumus's vast wealth, old-fashioned
piety, and locked wine cellars that Horace mocks tipsily—in his
role of "humble" client equalizing himself by the gift of a poem,
a gift more precious than any conventional one can be.

Augustus: The Great Patron

Among this society of amusing lovers and rich and powerful friends, of garden parties and dinners and pleasure, and the
ever-present thought of life's shortness and how it had been still
shorter for many before Augustus won, Horace had one more
great duty: the writing of odes for the new Great Patron. This
was the ethos of the new regime: Augustus prudently avoided
calling himself either king or perpetual dictator, the titles associ-
ated with the assassinated Julius Caesar, before his Roman subjects (though his Greek subjects called Augustus and his successors simply "the king" from the beginning). But whatever
titles he took in Rome or elsewhere, the genius of his system

was not to abolish the power of men like Dellius or Messalla, but to establish that from now on the emperor would be for everyone in the empire the patron above all patrons, the giver of gifts, the final court of all appeals. That required formal displays of gratitude for benefits received. Augustus required poems from his poets as much as he did gestures of reverence and worship for the privileges he bestowed on cities and citizens in the provinces. But both poets and subjects were supposed to invent the gestures themselves. The system of patronage kept its shape here too.

Horace's poems to Augustus are very different from those to his lovers and amici, but they are as personal and original, and as anchored in the real contemporary situation, as he can make them. The poems to Augustus in *Odes* 1–3 portray a regime that is brilliant in its promises and immensely successful so far, but new and still threatened. In most of them the poet portrays himself as one with the Roman people, praying, as he praises, for the stability of the new regime and the defeat of the chaos of the late Republic. When he speaks as the poet Horace individually, he speaks as a man whose personal life and career are committed to the success of the regime. In the greatest of the Roman Odes, 3.4, he goes the whole length of comparing Augustus's rise to power to his own ambitious rise from the Apulian countryside to his present poetic (and economic) eminence in Rome: if the muses aided him in this success they can help Augustus in the same way, difficult and doubtful as his task still is. In 3.25 Horace conjures up an ecstatic experience of the presence of the god Dionysus himself, and claims (the last mention of Caesar in the book) that the effort to sing Caesar's praises generated this experience. Of all the experiences he went through in writing lyric poetry, this took him the furthest.

That statement spoils an otherwise great poem to Dionysus for many a modern reader. Horace's odes in praise of the Augustan regime can easily be dismissed, and with some reason, as not poetry at all but arduous tours de force of imperial rhetoric, wrung from the poet against his grain by virtue of his position. They are, in fact, exactly that. But what makes them poetically interesting, in a way that the standard panegyrical language of the later, more established Roman Empire is not, is that Horace makes the arduousness and wringing obvious in the poems and doubly obvious in the context of the whole collection of odes. Along with brilliant praise of Augustus's achievements, his poems imply the precariousness of the regime, the ruler, and even of Maecenas's and some of his other noble addressees' positions. They proved somewhat intractable models for the poetry and prose of the later empire, in which the emperor and his projects are incapable of failure, his ministers incapable of ambiguity or disloyalty, and the panegyrist himself unequal to the task of describing such greatness. None of these pretences is in Horace; he describes in *Odes* 1–3 a regime still newly risen from a chaos that everyone remembers and to which Rome can still easily return.

In 23 B.C. the emperor had still not been seen much in Rome since Actium. Till August of 29 B.C. Octavian had spent his time determinedly touring the East to enlist all Antony's former allies among the cities and subject kings in his personal clientele. Then he returned and stayed in Rome long enough to lay down the new forms of government, to "restore the Republic," as he called it. One of the gifts he received for this action was his great name of Augustus, bestowed on him in January of 27 B.C. at the proposal of Munatius Plancus, himself a defector from Antony's ranks. After a whirlwind effort to restore Italian commerce and further his ambitious building programs in Rome, Augustus departed to subdue the native tribes of Spain in the years 26–24; for he was determined that the western, Latin-speaking part of his empire should be pacified and begin its progress to economic parity with the East. In this he was to be successful beyond belief. But in 23 this design was scarcely begun, though the already increasing prosperity of Italy in peace kept his popularity stable.

Illness attacked Augustus in Spain in 25 and 24, and again after he returned in 23, this time so seriously that he was forced to make deathbed provisions for Agrippa, Maecenas's rival, to succeed him. This was a blow to Maecenas's power at court, and the quarrels over the succession did not end there. Augustus's sister Octavia hoped that her son Marcellus, who was twenty, would be the successor, and Augustus had seemed to agree. He took Marcellus to Spain and married him to his daughter Julia.

Now, however, he was forced to confess that Marcellus was still too young, and that only Agrippa was as yet qualified to succeed him. But though Horace in the state odes makes one distant and respectful reference to Marcellus, whose short life was nearly over, there seems to have been no prospect of profit for Maecenas in following this prince's fortunes either.

Maecenas's circle was thus going through a tense period in 23, like the regime itself, and *Odes* 1–3 necessarily reflect this tension. The emperor valued praise from the established great poets of his regime, and there is no question that they had to give it in some form or another. Even those like Horace who approved of Augustus's regime found this a heavy and problematic task. One of the standard topics of Augustan verse is the *recusatio* or refusal. The poet sketches a few samples of wonderful things he might say about Augustus, then explains that his talents and verse are not up to a subject that only epic could celebrate. In ode 1.6 Horace brilliantly tries this one out on Agrippa instead ("my epic-writing friend Varius, a bird of broader wing, can sing your great deeds in peace and war"), the implied flattery being that Agrippa is the only person besides Augustus who is great enough to be spoken of with such reverence. But since Horace had picked up the lyre not merely of Sappho and Alcaeus but of Pindar, which had been used to celebrate the Olympic victories of kings, no such pretense was open to him. He had to be the *laudator* of the imperial *laudandus*.

Horace's odes to Augustus in the first book are written with an ingenuity and artifice that shows some strain. Odes 1.2 and 1.12 try the tack of distancing the subject of Augustus by means of ornamental mythology, which the poets of the court of Alexandria had known well how to do. In 1.2 Rome is said to have recently been so jolted by floods of the Tiber (which frequently damaged property and living quarters) that one might fear the age of Deucalion's flood has returned, and the fishes will dwell once more in the mountains and the deer swim. But the guilt from which the gods disdain to save us this time is the civil wars, which have left Rome depopulated. To what god will Jupiter give the "role" (*partis*, originally a role in a drama) of expiating this guilt and saving the collapsing empire? Apollo, or Venus, or Mars? Or will Mercury condescend to impersonate a youth on earth, as he does in Homer? But this time he will come as a youth who will "endure to be called" the avenger of Julius Caesar, win great triumphs, and stay on earth out of kindness far longer than a god would wish, to be the father of his people.

The epiphany of Augustus as Mercury, the Roman god of commerce and prosperity (for we know that in that guise Augustus was worshipped in Rome and elsewhere in Italy, first with him and then *as* him, Mercurius Augustus), is thus Horace's way of concluding this piece of poetic jewelry. To save us from flood, fire, destruction of property, and ruined neighborhoods, the god of business descends with winged feet, and the leading indicators are once more rising from their wartime lows. It was the sober truth. The complicated comedy coheres, the tone of mythological spoof in which the flood is described at the beginning, the descent of the god of property and prosperity at the end. But just barely.

This language of deification and emperor-worship (a poetic language, and reserved for lyric: Horace never bothers with it in the informal hexameter poems) is surprising in an ex-member of Brutus's army, but not that surprising. In odes like this Horace at least speaks not for the class of senatorial grandees and warlords among whom he had so many friends and patrons, but for the rest of the empire en masse. This is the language that many a Greek city-state and kingdom used toward Augustus, the new and beneficent, the personally attentive, the endlessly embassy-receiving and petition-answering Alexander of the Augustan Peace, whereas Alexander himself had merely conquered and died too young to organize and govern his conquests. It was the language of Italy, of the commercial classes, of the equestrian order; not just of men like Nasidienus, the hopeful equestrian dinner-giver, but of Maecenas and Horace themselves among the order's leaders and opinion-makers. It was what Tyndaris and Galatea and Lycidas wanted to hear: praise of the leader who wanted his eastern, Greek empire at last to forget war and the plundering habits of Roman senators, and bank its profits in peace.

This is how most modern historical scholarship has come to think of the difference between imperial and Republican Roman government and ideology, but it hasn't yet had its just impact on the criticism of Horace's and Vergil's state poetry. This poetry contrasts openly with the rest, but so did the Forum and the great temples to the state gods and the other government buildings contrast with the rest of the city. The state odes in Horace's poetic world do duty as a kind of downtown, official, governmental Rome that complements the portraits of the free private life around the piazzas and parks and in the great houses. In this section of his poems, Horace faced another great challenge to his powers as a poet, greater even than the private odes posed.

The second book gives us not praises of Caesar, but two odes that deal very wittily with the problem of writing state odes as Maecenas's circle saw it. The first of them is so audacious a piece of wit that its true meaning seems to have become clear only quite recently.

> Battering rainclouds do not always
> drench wheatfields, or whimsical
> gusts spatter the Caspian gulfs—
> not always. Ice does not remain,
> dear Valgius, solid in all seasons
> on the Armenian shore. The oaks
> on Garganus aren't always troubled,
> nor ashes widowed of leaves.
> You're always plying lost Mystes
> with tearful music; the evening star
> ascending finds your love ascendant,
> and the morning star that fades before
> the raging sun. Ancient Nestor,
> three times our age, did not forever
> mourn his good son; Troilus's parents
> and Phrygian sisters did not always
> weep for an adolescent. Leave, now,
> your soft laments, sing something new;
> monuments of Augustus Caesar,
> set up under Niphates' frozen
> cliffs; Euphrates, new to the role
> of subject river, cowed, subsiding;
> obedient Geloni riding,
> in strict bounds, their cold, small fields.   [*Odes* 2.9]

Since we no longer have Valgius's poems, we can't judge whether Mystes is dead or just off on a new affair and lost to Valgius, as more recent scholarship argues. In that case, Horace has sent his friend a "deepest sympathy in your hour of loss" card for rejection in love, not death, as at first appears. Or it may be that Mystes was understood in Maecenas's circle to have meant more after death to Valgius as a source of poetry than he had in real life. In any case, the tone of the poem is at first glance mournfully sympathetic—so sympathetic that it fooled many an earlier commentator completely with its sighs of "always . . . always . . . always," like something from a 1930s love song. At second glance, however, the poem is extremely ambiguous and ironic. What lover would be flattered to be compared to the thrice-decrepit Nestor mourning his young son Antilochus, or to Troilus's "parents and Phrygian sisters"? Again, Horace asks Valgius to exchange his frigid and watery topic—grief like a perpetual rainstorm or unending winter—for another frigid and watery but more imposing topic, the addition of various snows and rivers to the edge of Agrippa's and Strabo's imperialist war maps as Roman or Roman-controlled territory. "Frigid" and "watery" are both also terms of pure literary criticism in Horace's and Valgius's world. The irony is perfectly managed, perfectly in the tradition of sophisticated Alexandrian laureate poetry, like Callimachus's to the Ptolemies.

In *Odes* 2.12 Horace similarly jokes with Maecenas: Rome's wars with Hannibal, the myths of Hercules and the Titans (important reference points in the later Roman Odes)—are they or the wealth of Arabia really worth a golden lock of Licymnia's hair? But the theme cannot be put off forever. Book 3 at last gives in: here is the praise-poetry on the grand scale. The opening six poems of the book are all in Alcaics; they occupy 336 lines, exactly one-third of the book, and together they form the ensemble called the Roman Odes, Horace's most extended, explicit, and (for him) irony-free tribute to the new empire and its program.

Some of the six Roman Odes are not as good as others. The last ode is particularly hard to like. Till the temples of the gods are rebuilt, it begins (but Augustus, at great expense, already had rebuilt dozens), Rome is in danger, for its empire was built

on reverence for them. This should be a happy thought, for as
far as we can know the gods of Rome were now getting all the
sacrifices they deserved and more, to general approval. But this
is made to introduce the fatal topic of family life, of which
Horace draws two pictures: a negative one of present corruption
and a positive one of early rural virtue. Neglect of the gods leads
to scenes like this:

> The virgin, ripe for marriage, delights
> in learning Ionic dances, is full of artifice.
> Already with her whole being
> she dreams of forbidden lovers;
> will find ones younger than her husband
> while drinking his wine; she will not even
> pick one for quick and furtive favors
> given when all the lamps are doused,
> but in front of the guests, commanded, rises,
> with her husband's knowledge, whether a pedlar
> calls or a Spanish merchant captain,
> generous buyer of arts of shame!
> Not from such parents were the young men born
> who stained the sea with Punic blood,
> and brought down mighty Pyrrhus,
> dreadful Antiochus, dreadful Hannibal;
> but a masculine race of farmer's sons
> who learned to turn the earth with Sabine
> spades and to their stern mother's
> strict measurement hewed the logs
> and carried them till the sun altered
> the shape of shades on mountains, lifting
> the yoke from the tired bulls, bringing
> welcome rest as his chariot vanished.
> What have the ruinous years not made more small?
> Our parents' age was worse than our grandfathers',
> and we are worse, and bringing forth
> children more wicked still than we are.

[*Odes* 3.6.21–48]

Horace's feeling for the country saves the second picture to
an extent, but the mature virgin and her "Ionic" dances, and the

pedlar and ship captain, are to me the low point of all Roman poetry, because no lesser poet could have galvanized this plate of dead frogs' legs into so much rhetorical life. No doubt the virgin should walk over onto the next page and learn morals from Asterie, Gyges, and Enipeus! And that is a serious objection, too; Horace has not dared to introduce his Greek friends from the Campus Martius as threats to virtuous Roman marriage beds, as they certainly were, or the whole picture would be patently ridiculous even to him. Romans rich from the Spanish trade and Roman merchants are supposed to be somehow a wholly different kind of adulterers.

Thus the Roman Odes end, and very evidently on a note of loyalty rather than conviction. The fifth and sixth odes appeal to the people to raise themselves in the practice of military and private virtues to support the new regime, and are only partly successful even as rhetoric. The last stanza of ode 3.6, though, finishes them off on a note of warning that has its nobility. If the Augustan project fails, will it not be because the Romans can no longer create anything but another civil war in its wake? Less garish rhetoric would introduce that question better. But the suggestion may be made that there is a significant echo here. The last stanza translates the words of Astraea, who threatens the pastoral people of the Silver Age that she will depart as their vices bring on the Bronze Age. They come from the poem of Aratus on the constellations (ca. 280 b.c.), not much read now, but immensely familiar and beloved in Horace's day, both to poets, in the original Greek, and to Roman readers in the translation of Cicero: "Look what sort of race the fathers of the Golden Age left behind them, far meaner than themselves! But you will breed a viler still! Truly wars and unspeakable bloodshed shall come to mankind, and grievous woe shall be laid upon them" (Aratus *Phaenomena* 123–26).

If that echo sounds at the end in the silence, it well fits the presentation as a whole. For the two centerpieces to the Roman Odes, 3.3 and 3.4, have that same sense of urgency, of chaos and failure still untamed, and are (I think) both fine poems. The fourth ode especially, the longest and most ambitious lyric poem Horace ever wrote, is a triumphant success. My translation preserves the (intentionally) florid mythological baggage

and even the (intentionally) long-winded and pompous syntax,
to the extent that English will allow:

> Descend from heaven, royal Calliope,
> play on the flute a long-drawn tune,
> or to the strings of Apollo's lyre
> set flourishes of brilliant singing.
> Do you hear it? Or does some delightful
> madness delude me? I seem to wander
> through sacred groves that echo her
> in underflowing steams and breezes.
> When I was a child, a boy tired out
> with play, and sleeping, on the peak
> of Voltur in Apulia, outside
> my nurse's threshold, fabulous doves
> piled me with leaves, a famous wonder
> in Acerenza, nest for eagles,
> the glens of Banzi, and the level
> and fertile plains around Forenza,
> so no black vipers could disturb me,
> no bears, and nothing weigh me down
> but Apollo's laurel, Venus's myrtle,
> the gods' inspired, prophetic infant.   [*Odes* 3.4.1–20]

This is the tone of the first half, in which Horace establishes
that he is going to take up a theme of immemorial antiquity.
Poetry is the yoke-fellow of kingship and the order and peace of
society that kings achieve. The Muse Calliope is Augustus's
patron as much as she is Horace's own. But the development is
as daring as possible. It works in as much of Horace the present-
day Roman as the poem will take. Horace's amount of the
"myth" of his childhood (intentionally designed after a story
that bees fed the child Pindar with their honey) says that the
story spread all over Apulia, high (Acerenza, which is very high
in the Apulian mountains), middle (Banzi), and low-lying (Foren-
za). But his calling opened to him (lines 21–24) Roman fashionable resorts of the rich and noble: the Sabine country (high),
Tibur and Palestrina (further down), and (lowest-lying of all) the
shore resort of Baiae near Naples, famous and infamous for its
luxurious high-life.

Poetry has preserved Horace's life in war and peace with its magic sacredness. Moreover, it opens the whole map of Agrippa to him if he wishes: under the Muses' aegis he is safe throughout the world (lines 25–36). These lines *must* be here if the poem is not to be the Roman equivalent of antique-reproduction furniture: Horace *must* define himself as Horace, a lone poet of the modern world singing what is now self-consciously literature, not an ancient Greek poet singing with choruses to a whole society at the celebrations and dances for a king's victory in the games. Horace has only the model of his own success and riches, gained through poetry, to offer Augustus as an analogue for the primitive Greek notion expressed in Hesiod's *Theogony* (79–100) that poets and kings, as consolers of mankind's distress and creators of order in a chaotic world, are both the special care of Calliope. Horace is safe under her protection. But Augustus is not safe. He is worried and threatened and sick in the midst of his labors, only half accomplished, and the Muse can find words for him too, suggested by the ancient words of Hesiod:

> You heal Caesar, once the tired
> troops have been sent back to their villages;
> in your echoing sacred cavern
> you help him find relief from trouble.
> Motherly envoys, your gentle counsel
> refreshes him, rejoices you.
> Both you and I know this: The godless
> Titans fell by his rain of lightning
> who governs the brute earth, the sea
> and wind, the cities of men, the kingdom
> of ghosts, gods and mortals together,
> equally ruling, the One Commander.
> . . . .
> What was Typhoeus, what was Mimas,
> what was the the empty, threatening stance of
> Porphyrion, or the torn-up tree trunks
> that made Enceladus's javelins,
> to the loud-cymbaling shield of Pallas?
> To greedy Vulcan here, the matron Juno
> there, or the god whose bow

is never taken from his shoulders,
who dips his long hair loose in the cold dew
of Delphi, and who rules the thickets
of wolfish Lycia, and the groves
of Delos where he was born: Apollo?
Might without mind falls of its own weight.
Might and sobriety the gods
push forward, onward; scorn and spurn
might without limit, criminal, soulless:
I draw this moral, witness Gyas
the hundred-handed, and Orion,
attempter of Diana's glory,
felled by a maiden's delicate arrow.
The earth wails as monsters fall
upon her, mourns her children, glowing
with lightning still in lurid Orcus.
They breathe fire, but Aetna stands
unmoved, their prison, and the eagle's
beak is still fixed in Tityos's liver;
on amorous Pirithoos
hundreds of chains are piled, and hold.

[*Odes* 3.4.37–48 and 53–80]

Horace has daringly taken his theme from the first Pythian Ode (474 B.C.), the crown of all Pindar's work. This had been addressed to Hiero, king of Syracuse, who at that time dominated Sicily, the land of the volcanoes, and whose volcanic and turbulent populace was to overthrow his dynasty not long after the ode was written.

In Pindar's poem, the vision of order that the lyre conjures for the benefit of the king and chariot victor is throughout suggestive of continuing threat, of order hard-won. Zeus and his children, the lovers of the lyre, are safe in their palace where the eagle of Zeus sleeps by his throne to its happy strains. But "those that are not among Zeus's allies are in torment at the cry of the lyre." Typhoeus still rages under the volcanoes of Sicily, and Hiero's subjects are not a docile race. King Hiero is Zeus on earth for now, but also, even physically, a sick and tormented man like the Sophoclean hero Philoctetes, to whom Pindar implicitly compares him in the poem. The order that Hiero and his son hope to achieve now that the barbarians are defeated will require much wise counsel and wariness to succeed and endure; that is the note on which Pindar concludes.

Horace softens this picture, but not entirely. Augustus has finished one work of peace, the discharging of the legions to their farmland, but others wait. The picture Horace gives as parallel is not of the Olympians at last feasting in triumph, but of their awesome calm in battle; and particularly the portrait of Apollo amid the strife, too calm even to be ruffled, as if he were about to wash his hair in cold water; like the Apollo amid Centaurs and Lapiths, tranquilly stretching out his arm over their battle, on the west front of the fifth-century temple of Zeus at Olympia. Apollo does not need to exert himself; "might without mind falls of its own weight."

The poem is a success, though a dangerous and difficult one. (Significantly, Horace has to confine his Pindaric imitation to half the poem, forty lines, a fraction of the length of the original.) This is partly because it embodies a determination Horace must have made early and kept—that he was going to address his state poetry to the imperial statue and image, the symbol of order, and not to Augustus the man—and partly because of its vivid suggestion of order genuinely threatened. The Titans and Giants in ancient sculpture, as in Hesiod's and Pindar's poems, are used to symbolize threats that nearly brought a city or a nation down, as the Titans nearly brought down the gods themselves. They are significantly *not* a common topic of imperial flattery after this time. Later poets shrank from exalting the emperor's enemies so high.

Even at that, most readers notice with pleasure that several poems later, in 3.14, as if reflecting on his exhausting task, Horace lays out a few more complex verses on Augustus's return from Spain in 24. They indicate for anyone to see that he is conscious of having been on both sides, like so many of his patrons. Horace purposefully begins by appealing over the heads of the aristocracy to the common people, where Augustus's real support lay. "Caesar, O plebeians! just now said to have sought in Hercules' style the laurel whose price is death, returns home from the Spanish shore. May his wife, rejoicing in her distinguished husband, come forth sacrificing to the just gods, and the sister of our great leader. . . . This holiday shall truly take away my black worries; as long as Caesar reigns over the world I shall fear neither riot nor death by violence." Very direct; that *was* the fear, and would be once more if Augustus died and chaos came again. Horace alludes to the gloomy history of so many past decades: "Go, servant, and find perfumed oil and garlands, and a cask that remembers the Marsic War, if there are any that escaped the wanderings of Spartacus. And tell Neaera to come too, but if her doorkeeper stops you, let that go. Graying hair softens the spirit that once was so eager for quarrels and complaints; I wouldn't have taken that in my hot youth, when Plancus was consul." But Munatius Plancus's consulship was in the year of Philippi. Once Horace would never have taken part in a festival to welcome a dictator home.

What has convinced him is peace. Horace's praise-poems were addressed not to the man but to the imperial image, at whose feet from now till the end of the empire citizens and even slaves could lay petitions that officials were obliged by law to send to the palace itself; and not to the imperial image after all, but to the best of the things it symbolized, the Augustan Peace. The emperor and all his family (the "wife," the "sister") figure in Horace's poetry as nothing but images, seen only by their impact on society and on other people he addresses more directly.

Licinius Murena and Maecenas

Nor, to return to Horace's circle of lesser friends and patrons for one last set of poems, is this impact always beneficent. In 23 Maecenas's role in the regime was being undermined not just by the ascendancy of Agrippa, but by trouble between his brother-in-law Licinius Varro Murena and Augustus. Not long after the publication of *Odes* 1–3, Varro was arrested and killed for conspiring against Augustus's life. In 25 Varro won a great victory against the Salassi who infested northwest Italy near the Alps, and forty-four thousand of them were sold into slavery. In July of the next year he was designated consul with the emperor for 23, and perhaps lasted long enough to be inaugurated in January 23; however, his name was canceled from the consular lists and a Calpurnius Piso took his place. Maecenas's influence in the regime was badly damaged by this event, supposedly because he betrayed to Terentia the secret that her brother's life was in danger.

The chronology of these events is uncertain and mysterious in the extreme, but that they have their impact on *Odes* 1–3 there is no longer much doubt. Horace addresses an ode to Maecenas's brother-in-law that jumps out of the context of the other odes and strikes home like a snake with its swiftness and terrible urgency. There is no time for once to invite the addressee to wine parties and to give him gentle and indirect counsel; not is there any time for subtle structures and unexpected contrasts, for ornament and periodic rhetoric, but only for one point, to be driven home in a series of blunt, short sentences. Licinius Varro Murena's house philosophers, who played the same role for princely Roman establishments as domestic chaplains once did in English country houses, are known to have been Aristotelians. Horace drives home the Aristotelian idea of the golden mean between extremes as the foundation of the virtues, not smilingly, as earlier in the *Satires*, but as urgently as if he were wrestling for a soul on its deathbed:

> You will live more correctly, Licinius,
> neither courting high seas, nor, too cautious
> of every gale, risking your keel
> close to the shore.
> Between extremes, the middle is golden.
> Keep safe away from the run-down hut,
> keep soberly from the towering hall
> that all men envy.
> The winds tear at the tall pine
> more often, and the high towers
> make the worst ruins: it is the peak
> that lightning hits.
> The prudent heart fears on a good day,
> hopes on a bad day, for what must come,
> a change. The sky-god brings back in
> the ugly winter,
> then leads us past it. If things are bad now,

> someday they won't be. Apollo awakens
> the silent lyre's music; not always
> is it the bowstring
> he tightens. Tight places demand strength
> and high spirits. It's the same wisdom
> as reefing, when the wind's too helpful,
> your puffed-out sails.   [*Odes* 2.10]

The imperial statue of Apollo can come as terrifyingly alive with either of its attributes, lyre or weapon, as the statue of Venus-Hathor can come comically alive with her whip. This is the ode in which Horace's phrase *aurea mediocritas*, so often derided, occurs; but it is pretty impressive in context: "The middle way can be golden in a situation of ultimate risk like yours." Why say this in public, when it could (and must) have been said in private? Did Maecenas and his circle urgently need this to be said to distance themselves from what were already known to be Varro Murena's problems? No certain answer can be given, but the ode illustrates the side of Augustus's court that could suddenly become like those of the Visconti or the Gonzagas in Renaissance Italy. It was (as throughout the empire) the senators and generals who were at risk, not the people, and their fall was for the most part received with indifference or hostility in the streets. The statesmen of the Renaissance valued this poem highly, and for good reasons. (Its first translator into English, Henry Howard, earl of Surrey, was beheaded for treason by Henry VIII.)

Beyond a doubt, uncertainties like this in the situation of the 20s B.C. give a yet brighter color to some of Horace's great poems to Maecenas. Throughout the collection, ever more powerfully, Horace develops the theme that he, at the Sabine farm, can be not a client but a patron to Maecenas, conferring relief for both his imaginary hypochondria and his real political worries.

The Sabine farm, the place of art and contemplation, provides rest and safety throughout the *Odes* from all kinds of strife—from the summer heat and from danger to the flocks, from the evil passions of Tyndaris's lover, most of all from Rome and its too-high-piled grandeur and political dangers. All this is exquisitely put into one famous poem in book 3:

O fountain of Bandusia, clearer, brighter
than crystal, fit to be given fragrant wine
and flowers, tomorrow a young goat's yours.
His forehead budding with new horns
predestines him to sex and battles
in vain; his blood will stain with scarlet
your cold flow, poor offspring
of my lust-heated herd! The savage
time of the dogstar cannot warm you;
you offer still delicious coldness
to my bulls, tired from the ploughing,
to my flock, straying in from sunheat.
You will join the renowned and noble fountains,
when my song tells of the ilex, straddling
the hollow rocks, from which your waters
leap, with their endless voices, down.   [*Odes* 3.13]

Horace is talking about a real fountain, almost certainly at
his farm. But more than a fountain is meant: the Callimachean
"pure fountain" of poetry is symbolized here. The bloodshed is
the sacrifice of reality to create art from it, the fountain is a
natural object from which art is created. (That is why it draws to
itself one of Horace's few superlatives or superlative-like expressions: normally Horace avoids clichés like "whiter than
snow" as firmly as the superlative itself, but "clearer than [artif-
icial] crystal" makes exactly the point he wants.) Horace, as poet
and patron, is the creator of a "noble" fountain, the equal of the
sacred poetic fountains of Greece. The heat and turmoil of life
symbolized by the summer disappear into it, into poetry, and
emerge refreshed. Greatness and littleness are measured differently here: in the country art comes into its own, consoles, re-
freshes, gives life.

It seems we are intended to have read this poem before we
come to the great ode 3.29 to Maecenas, the last poem in the
collection proper (only an epilogue, another triumph-ode to
Horace's achievement itself, remains). Maecenas and his troubles: Rome in the dogdays of a hot summer, the too-grand palace, the political worries, may all be plunged in this fountain,
and emerge not just refreshed but defiant of all that may come.

Here I have no reason to risk the poem's effect, for the reader without Latin, by any verses of my own. I quote instead part of Dryden's version, the greatest Horatian translation in the English language:

> Descended of an ancient time
> That long the Tuscan scepter swayed,
> Make haste to meet the generous wine,
> Whose piercing is for thee delayed:
> The rosy wreath is ready made,
> And artful hands prepare
> The fragrant Syrian oil, that shall perfume thy hair.
> . . . .
> Make haste and come;
> Come, and forsake thy cloying store;
>   Thy turret, that surveys, from high,
> The smoke, and wealth, and noise of Rome,
> And all the busy pageantry
> That wise men scorn, and fools adore;
> Come, give thy soul a loose, and taste the pleasures
> of the poor.
> . . . .
> The Sun is in the Lion mounted high;
>   The Syrian star
>   Barks from afar,
> And with his sultry breath infects the sky;
> The ground below is parched, the heavens above us
> fry;
>   The shepherd drives his fainting flock
>   Beneath the covert of a rock,
>   And seeks refreshing rivulets nigh.
> . . . .
> Enjoy the present smiling hour,
> And put it out of Fortune's power;
> The tide of business, like the running stream,
> Is sometimes high, and sometimes low,
> A quiet ebb, or a tempestuous flow,
> And always in extreme.
> . . . .

Happy the man, and happy he alone,
He, who can call today his own;
He who, secure within, can say,
"To-morrow do thy worst, for I have lived today;
Be fair or foul, or rain, or shine,
The joys I have possessed, in spite of fate, are mine;
Not heaven itself upon the past has power,
But what has been, has been, and I have had my
   hour."

One could compare the fountain-poem to a Japanese fan folded up so that as little as possible is seen; the great Maecenas ode is the same fan, folded out to its maximum extent. Of all the gift-poems and consolations offered to a patron in the three books of odes, this last becomes the greatest. Both by its position in the collection and by its own weight and grandeur, it overshadows even the great Pindaric centerpiece of the Roman Odes, and not by accident. The imperial image cannot be asked out to country houses, and in this poem the patron's troubles do not have to be veiled in a statuary group of gods and Titans. The parts of the poem that are "about" Horace and the addressee do not need to be so disjoined, for Maecenas and he are friends and equals. Amid the cool fountains, there is refuge first from the summer, then from all the strife that besets Maecenas's soul from all over the imperial map—all this if he will condescend to become an equal for a moment, his client's client. And from that process, though one thought there was only poetry there, one learns the wisdom of the Stoics itself: to fall back on integrity in pure solitude, the imperturbable calm of the wise man before the storm.

Horace's position, which he works out explicitly in the first book of epistles (and may have had already in mind when he published this poem) is that though all religions and philosophies are matters of debate among which one can wander uncommitted, that moral absolutism which he mocked in the *Satires*, and which is the peculiar note of Stoicism, must be somewhere in even the least "committed" man's armory. And since the Stoics claimed this attitude was life "according to nature," the Sabine farm is part proof that they were right: such thoughts breathe through the trees and rustle through the Bandusian spring, even if Rome drowns them out. They give one the strength even to contemplate giving up the trees and the spring themselves and sailing off relying on one's own independent self, if fate, or the patron, or even the emperor force one to do so. The one thing in Dryden's translation that I have to correct is the phrase "not heaven itself": Horace more daringly writes "not Jove himself." Augustus lurks too often behind the word *Jove* in the *Odes* to be entirely absent here. In 3.4 (a similar consolation from poet to patron in difficulties, but much less personal in its tone about the patron), all Augustus's enemies are collapsed into allegory as Titans and ambitious amorous heroes. Here, with greater realism, the thought of political dangers to Maecenas from the one palace more powerful, if not more brilliant, than his own leads into an ultimate general statement: Jove himself cannot take from me the life I have *lived*—let alone the world, let alone Augustus.

Some Touches of Solitude

Only a few poems that illustrate major themes in the ensemble of *Odes* 1–3 have been used here. There are poems that do not fit these themes: the larger structure has plenty of space for poems that don't "belong." Some of the best of them take up themes that are unexpected in Horace: mystical religious experience, death not conceived as a theme between friends and lovers but purely as the experience of final futility and loneliness.

In 2.28, a disembodied voice addresses the long-dead Pythagorean astronomer of the fourth century B.C., Archytas of Tarentum, and dwells on the futility of both his mystic philosophy of reincarnation and his knowledge of mathematics and astronomy:

> The barest funeral gift, a little dust, by the Matine
> shore
> confines you now, Archytas, measurer
> of sea and land and the sands never before
> numbered.   [*Odes* 1.28.1–3]

The disembodied address is opulently developed for twenty lines, and then there is a sudden, wrenching twist. The speech on the futility of wisdom turns out to be the silent, imagined prayer of a corpse, cast up on shore from a shipwreck and forlornly begging the passerby, if he fears its curse, for the same handful of dust as sufficed to lay Archytas to rest. Only a couple of place names (Venusia, Tarentum) even hint that the poet pictures himself as the passerby, traveling down the shore near his birthplace and his favorite southern resort. The "themes" are deliberately out of the ordinary: no patrons or lovers to share thoughts with, no stanzas on the futility of ownership or on death looming behind love, or the shoring of poetic monuments against ruin. The poem contemplates for once the futility even of all wisdom, before the bare fact of the drowned corpse, contemplated in solitude, "speaking" to the poet this way without eliciting a word in reply.

The mystical experience turns out to be the writing of poems like these. It drives Horace twice to compose hymns to Dionysus (2.19, 3.25) to express his sense of having reached places in his own mind that the *Epodes* and *Satires* had never touched. In these poems he recurs to the last source one would expect of him (it also supplies the climax of the first book of epistles): Euripides' *Bacchae*. Here he seems to have caught many of his admirers off guard, even convinced them that he believed in "the gods" for a moment:

> Dionysus! I saw him, teaching songs
> on far-away cliffs, believe me, future
> world; the memorizing Nymphs,
> the goatfoot Satyrs' ears erected.
> *Euoi*, the mind shivers with fear again,
> and full of him the heart, unsteady,
> rejoices: *euoi*, spare me, Bacchus,
> spare me, god of the heavy thyrsus,
> of terror. He answers. Enduring Bacchae,
> fountains of wine, rivers that turn to
> udders of milk, and streams of honey
> that flow from hollow treetrunks, I

sing back: and blessed Ariadne's
crown made a constellation, Pentheus's
palace split with tremendous ruin,
Lycurgus torn on Thracian beaches.
You turn back rivers, turn the barbaric sea;
drunk in the sheer and lonely rockface,
you tie with snakes, as if with wool
fillets, the Maenads' harmless tresses.
You, your father's kingdoms' heights
scaled by squadrons of reckless Titans,
twisted Rhoetus back with the claws
of a lion, with its tremendous jaws:
though for your love of jokes and dances
and games you had not been considered
a force in battle: but you were
the same in peace, the same in combat.
Cerberus saw you with your golden
horn of wine and wagged his tail,
harmless; and as you left, with triple
mouth lapped at your legs, your toes.   [*Odes* 2.19]

Many scholars who did not believe the black-legged swan of 2.20 have taken this poem seriously. But they have interpreted it as a religious experience of Horace's in real life and time, whereas it is about the lonely, Dionysiac experience of creativity: "The artist is the most interesting of all creatures, for he represents creativity, the definition of man." Horace can say that in verse only by representing himself, first learning from and then (as the orthodox teaching went) *becoming* Dionysus, and driving the moral home again with unsurpassed power in the calmer world of the *Epistles* (1.16.72–79). His poems were his own lonely battle with the Titans, and he too won.

These poems reassure the reader: the fountain and the farm are indeed symbols of a deeper center of consciousness that exists by itself. They give meaning and authority to the intensely societal tone of the rest. All Horace's poetry is the poetry of an unmarried man in an intensely familial society whose cant (like ours today) was that the family should somehow be "restored." But as for us it was only taking new forms, freer and happier ones, and Horace is at his least convincing in the Roman Ode 3.6 when he dutifully claims that the same happy, bickering life that Greek men and women lead in the next poem is the source of all evils for Romans. The world he pictures is an interconnected family throughout, because of its strong relationships, its familial networks of clients and patrons, beginning from the friends and lovers meeting in the crowded streets and on the Campus and ending in the formal celebrations of the Great Family, the State, and the Great Patron, Augustus.

Horace's picture of that society in what one would have thought was the least appropriate genre, lyric verse, is much fuller and more honest and detailed than it has usually been taken to be. It surprises and delights me to notice that Sir Maurice Bowra, at the end of one of the best short essays ever written on the *Odes* as pure poetry, says that "the four books of the Odes, with their hundred and three short poems, cover *a wider range of experience* and present it in a more satisfying form than almost any other comparable book written by man" (emphasis mine).*

These are not words one would have expected from a Pindarist, but they show why Horace felt confident in concluding this collection of odes not with Augustus, nor Maecenas, but with himself once more, and by elaborating an image of the utmost liveliness and contemporaneity for Romans, if not for us: *exegi monumentum*, "I have built [my] monument." People not much above Horace in rank were building ever more extravagant funeral monuments to themselves and their families even as he wrote, and while they lived. The immense pyramid of Cestius in Rome and the yet-more-tremendous monument of Horace's friend Plancus, a sort of marble water tank visible for many miles on its high hill in Gaeta, are still among the more memorable sites of anyone's tour of Italy. The mausoleum that Augustus had already built for himself and his family still takes up in its ruins an entire large public square in modern Rome. To us it seems a mere joke when an American expresses his "personality" in a funeral monument, burying himself under a concrete life-size Mercedes or an enormous golf ball, but Romans

*"The Odes of Horace," in Cyril Connolly, ed., *The Golden Horizon* (London, 1953), p. 454.

were not afraid to design in detail everything they wanted remembered of themselves—even to express the most baroque whims—in their monuments. Horace therefore never fuses more perfectly a common feeling of his people with a standard poetic theme—that of poetic immortality—than when he ends the collection by characterizing it as a monument greater than all the pretentious buildings of his age:

> I have built a monument more lasting than bronze,
> that looms above royal deserted pyramids,
> that no eroding rain nor raving wind
> can ever crumble, nor the unnumbered
> series of years, the flight of generations.
> I shall not wholly die; my greater part
> escapes the poor goddess of funerals, growing
> in posthumous praise so long as pontifex
> and silent virgin still ascend the Capitol.
> In my homeland where the Aufidus roars with
>   freshets,
> where Daunus rose to rule his parched kingdom
> of farmers, humble once, then powerful,
> and princely, I will be called the first to bring
> Aeolian singing into Italian music.
> Invest yourself in the pride you bought
> with your own merit, graciously bind
> my hair, Melpomene, with Delphic laurel.   [*Odes* 3.30]

IV LATER LIFE AND WORKS

Epistles 1

Horace devoted the three years after the publication of *Odes* 1–3 to a book of twenty poems, imaginary letters, in the same conversational hexameter verse as his earlier *Satires*. The first book of epistles is an even more subtle exercise than the *Satires* in the composition of poems that both make sense in themselves and gain immensely in power and force if read as a series from beginning to end. Its unity comes from four beautifully interwoven running themes.

The first is the study of philosophy. In the first two long epistles to Maecenas and Lollius, Horace announces himself as returning, now he is forty-five, to the philosophical books and even the Homeric poems that he studied in his youth, in search of wisdom. Can Horace find by himself the lonely wisdom of the Wise Man? The answer is joking, ambiguous, ironical, at least to a certain point. Horace makes the reader follow him through many changes of mind and many relapses, but not forever. When he finally arrives at a formulation of what personal independence and integrity mean to him in epistles 1.16–18, the effect is all the more impressive for the many backtrackings and blind alleys that preceded it, but really foreshadowed it from the first.

Horace relies here on the ambiguities suggested by the sort of ancient philosophical summary called "doxography." After so many schools of philosophy had covered the same ground and contradicted themselves and one another, many Greeks and Romans of Horace's day fell back on what Phillip K. De Lacy has called the search for "disjunctive truth." On immortality, for example, we may know that either we fall into an eternal sleep or there is a reward for the just man after death, as

Socrates explained in the *Apology*, and we may prepare our-
selves for both. Whichever is true, no other possibility exists.
On most subjects a philosopher considers, the list of variant
opinions in antiquity was of course much longer. This kind of
search, not so much for certainty as for the exhaustion of possibilities ("the truth is somewhere in this list"), was aided by the
composition of doxographies. Doxographers, like the great
Arius Didymus in Augustus's day, compiled lists of the opinions of leading authorities on pleasure vs. virtue, the extent to
which the happiness of the wise could be damaged by pain or
misfortune, the shape of the cosmos, and so forth ("Thales believed . . . Plato believed . . . the Aristotelians . . . the Stoics
hold . . . the Epicureans teach that . . . "). Their readers would
thus be apprised of all possible answers and could prepare for
any one of them to turn out to be correct.

Horace turns the study of such dry lists into a spectacular
drama of ever-wavering search that takes place in his own life,
and combines it with a second theme: that of place. He is in
Rome or at the Sabine farm or considering various options for
travel as he writes one or the other of the epistles. The places
themselves, by their suggestions of what the good life might be,
shift his attention on the doxographical page from one column
to another. The Sabine farm suggests various choices in the list
of possibilities that other places do not: the simple pleasures of
the Epicurean, the independence and absolutism of the Stoic.
Rome and the resort towns and the villas of his rich friends
suggest hedonism or distraction and confusion of values. The
outer edges of the imperial map are not left out. In epistles 1.3,
1.8, 1.9, and 1.11, letters are sent out to Tiberius and his suite of
literary men and court officials as they travel from Thrace east-
wards. Then at the end of epistle 1.12 a friend in Sicily is advised, by way of giving him the latest news from Rome, that
Agrippa has pacified Spain, Tiberius has received the submission of Armenia and Parthia, and the prosperity of Italy has
never seemed greater. The book thus dates itself as published
about the time (20 B.C.) that Tiberius concluded a peace in the
East with the Parthians, to general rejoicing. Horace moves
round various places throughout the book. He sends his letters

various distances, ranging from a same-day dinner invitation sent across the city, to letters sent far away to Tiberius and the East. As Horace moves and his addressees move, his choices on the doxographical page vary. But the choices start to find limits, move toward resolution and commitment, as the poems concentrate more and more on the Sabine farm.

The third major theme is friendship, not (once more) anything like what we call friendship, but *amicitia*, the system of clientage, patronage, and action for mutual benefit that was Roman male society—a system Horace has risen through and seen, as he thinks, all round. Can Horace make himself wise enough, as he tries his various shifting grounds, to equalize his relationship to all these amici? The answer to this question shifts back and forth from self-doubt to defiance throughout the book. But here too the final answer is more positive and self-assured than could have been expected even from the earlier poetry. At least four epistles in book 1 (7, 16, 17, 18) deal at length with the possibility that the whole patronage system that Horace posed earlier as accepting is so damaging to the client's character and integrity that he would be better off stepping out of it into poverty and solitude—even, if necessary as a last resort, suicide.

In 1.7, for example, this "defiant" tendency reaches a first climax (a much greater is to come in 1.16–18). Maecenas himself is told to "take back your Sabine farm" if the price is attendance on his whims in Rome in the middle of the August heat. Horace's health will not stand it; he intends to winter by the sea and will see Maecenas no earlier than next spring.

> If you want me always attending you, give me back
> a young, strong body, a low, black forehead of curls,
> a fresh, young voice, and a fine-looking, open-
>   mouthed laugh,
> and real grief, over wine, when audacious Cinara left
>   us.   [*Epistles* 1.7.25–29]

Does Maecenas, he asks, think of his client as being like the fox in the fable that got fat in the granary and now can't get out by the hole that let him in?

> If that image appeals to you, I resign your gifts every
>   one.
> I don't praise the sleep of the poor and just, when I'm
>   stuffed
> myself with foie gras, and I wouldn't change my
>   freedom
> and leisure for the gold of Arabia. You call me honest
> and like me for it, and I call you "my prince and my
>   father"
> to your face, and say the exact same thing when
>   you're gone.
> See, then, if I can't give all your gifts back and enjoy
>   it!   [34–39]

He tells Maecenas the fable of a humble auctioneer (of his
own father's rank, but that is left unsaid) who was "taken up"
by a witty nobleman who found him amusing. The nobleman
was Marcius Philippus, consul in 91 B.C., whose son was Augustus's stepfather. In the end Philippus helped the humble
auctioneer Volteius to buy a Sabine farm, and offered loans to
keep it going. When things started to go disastrously wrong, the
auctioneer found that the noble Philippus knew all along he
wasn't up to the work and troubles of farming, and was merely
playing with him. In the end Volteius is reduced to begging
Philippus to be given back his former life. Horace implies that he
would as soon give back the Sabine farm and do the same:

> When a man has seen how much better's the life he
>   left
> than the life he sought, he should double back and
>   start over.
> Each must gauge himself by his own yardstick and
>   rule.   [96–98]

This is of course not to be mistaken for a real letter to
Maecenas. It is a work of art, a gift to him. To publish it is public
praise of Maecenas's love of freedom and originality in his
friends. Maecenas was nothing if not easily bored with the obvious in art. If we compare the praise of Maecenas and his circle
"artfully" inserted in the satire about the bore, 1.9, it seems

even a little coarse compared to this. "You praise me for my truthfulness, and I say to others, the same as to you, that you are my prince, my father." As one looks twice at that statement, it becomes much more prominent in the poem than it looked at first.

The poem is still astonishing: "Take back the Sabine farm itself, if the price of attendance on you is to be my health and my leisure," Horace seems to say. "See, then, if I can't give all your gifts back and enjoy it!" In epistle 1.16 Horace builds to a still more astonishing climax: he advises a young nobleman in Rome that he cannot find the truth about himself from his clients' flattery. He pictures the Sabine farm, in contrast to the city, as a sort of ground of being from which one can learn that only a man prepared to defy the king himself at the cost of his life is a man of integrity. The king is Pentheus in Euripides' *Bacchae*, but he is by implication a symbol of Augustus: a wise man must be able to face down, at least theoretically, not only Maecenas but the Great Patron of the empire to keep his integrity. From that high ground Horace advises two young men starting their careers in Rome, in epistles 1.17 and 1.18, that a client's life, whether his own position is humble or high, involves some sacrifice of integrity at every point. Independence may be the goal of participating in the system, but it is nowhere found in the process of winning it. Participation is best justified by the reflection that keeping one's integrity from the start would involve abandoning self-realization in society and winning nothing at all; but it is a question whether a man who can be contented with a mere competence would not be as well sitting out the whole game on the sidelines, since the best thing you win is independence and a competence anyway.

All these themes are intimately involved with the fourth: growing older. Forty-five, in the Romans' short-lived society, was the point of transition from *iuvenis* to *senior*. The first lines of the book complain that Horace is a retired gladiator, an aging racehorse, not young enough to obey Maecenas's command and compete once more before the literary public. The last lines treat his book humorously as a foolish client of Horace's own, a young and beautiful freedman newly liberated, reluctantly dismissed into publication. Horace, older and disillusioned, mocks

its youthful hopes of adventure and commands it at least to tell
its readers some things about its patron: the last detail, on which
the book ends, is that the author was near forty-five when he
wrote it. In epistle 1.14 he tells the slave-manager of his Sabine
farm why he now prefers the farm to Rome:

> I, who gloried in fine togas and perfumed hair,
> whom you know expensive Cinara loved for free,
> who was tipsy on pure Falernian all afternoon,
> abridge my dinners and nap on the grass by the
>   stream,
> not ashamed I had fun, but ashamed not to quit it
>   now.   [*Epistles* 1.14.32–36]

This picture of a man feeling his age more deeply than had
the poet of the *Odes* goes along with further kinds of life-review,
to borrow a term from modern psychologists of aging, that
shape the themes of patronage, places, philosophy. Horace declares himself client emeritus at forty-five and reviews his whole
experience of the patronage system with astonishing honesty
from outside. One by one he reconsiders places in the light of
experience so far: Rome, the Sabine farm, the resorts and villas
of favorite vacation places like Baiae, Tarentum, Salerno, even
Thrace and Asia Minor, once the scene of his youthful campaigns with Brutus, across which Tiberius and his suite are now
traveling to their meeting with the representatives of the East.
Above all he finds himself rereading his books of philosophy
and poetry with a new understanding that was not there in his
youth, seeking in them what is really valuable in the light of
experience.

The first poem contains all four themes at once. Horace,
having grown older, is trying to find himself among the contradictory philosophies of life he knows. But Rome, with its concentration on materialism and money making, is no place for
such studies, and Maecenas, as patron, wants too much of him,
interrupts him, imposes values on him that are social, not real,
when a true friend would help him be wise:

> You were sung in my first Latin verses, will be sung
>   in the last:

> but I have my wooden sword, I've performed long
>   enough,
> Maecenas; you want to confine me again to the games
> of long ago. I'm not of that age, nor mind.
>
> [*Epistles* 1.1.1–4]

Horace is an old racehorse who would "break his sides" if he tried, a gladiator who has been given the wooden sword and retired. In addition, he has laid aside verses permanently (a running joke: he's of course "obeying" the "command" and writing verse as he says this) for the study of philosophy. Horace's search for wisdom is puzzling him: now he "belongs" to one school and now to another. He is frantic at everything that keeps him from finding out "what that is that profits the poor man and rich man alike, and, ignored, is equally hurtful to boys and old men." What "that" might be, though, is (supposedly) still perfectly unclear to him.

But he feels, by instinct, that just as a man his age does not exercise to be an Olympic athlete, or anoint his eye infection with the purpose of acquiring the eyesight of a lynx, so also even the "elementary" part of philosophy can make him better, if not give him certainty. Memories of childhood, as he reviews his life and remembers his boyhood in the city, remind Horace that the elementary education of the Roman people is business. It teaches that money is everything, no matter whether it came to you honestly or dishonestly. That is why Roman life has no fixed purpose, is all confusion and self-contradiction. Only the game in which he and the other Roman children sang "You'll be king if you do right; if you don't, you won't be king" told the truth in that world. Then he turns once again on Maecenas:

> If I come to you with a cheap and lopsided haircut,
> you laugh. If my under-tunic's as old and worn
> as my over-tunic's fresh, if my toga's on wrong,
> you laugh. But what if my thought wars with itself,
> spurns what it sought for, grabs what it just left aside,
> spins crazily, fails of coherence through all of my life,
> tears down and builds up and confuses the round and
>   the square?

You think, "That's the normal craziness," and you
    don't laugh,
nor tell me I need a doctor, nor ask the lawcourts
to assign me a guardian, though you're my fortress in
    life,
and are full of bile at the ill-cut fingernails
of a friend who depends on you, respects you, looks
    only to you.
In sum, the wise man is God's inferior only;
he alone is rich, free, powerful, beautiful, king
of kings, and the standard of health—when he hasn't
    the grippe.   [*Epistles* 1.1.94–108]

Friend: respected client: amicus. Horace has once more inserted the brilliant compliments, the acquiescence in writing
under Maecenas's patronage, into the context of the "free man's
complaint." And his search through the doxographies has not
given him any more certainty—so far—than Maecenas's. But if
we trace Horace's thought further, especially in the second half
of the book, we find that it does indeed arrive at certainties,
even if only with the help of places. The climax of Horace's
confusion and sickness in 1.8 is to want to be in Rome when he
is at the farm and at the farm when he is in Rome, and that is not
accidental. The whole movement of the book is, in place, toward
the Sabine farm, and in philosophy, toward the same final
choice of Stoic moral absolutism as an ultimate focal point as the
farm suggested in *Odes* 3.29.

Epistles 1.10–15 might be called all Sabine in tone; that is to
say, the oscillations around the doxographical page start favor-
ing simplicity, absolutism, and Stoicism, as the place, the Sabine
farm, starts to be more and more clearly the center of Horace's
consciousness insofar as he is a Wise Man at all. It is as if in the
course of his life-review at forty-five he looked back at his own
youthful satires and found the Stoic philosophy of Stertinius,
"Mr. Snore," and "Crispinus's janitor" not so totally ridiculous
after all. That is predicted from the beginning. The tone of the
joke about the Wise Man's cold at the end of epistle 1.1, compared to the running end-jokes about Stoicism in the first three
satires of the first book, is less contemptuous. (Horace himself

has tried and failed to learn the Stoic Wise Man's secret, but he
doesn't claim any longer that there is no such thing.) As the
scene starts to be more and more fixed on the Sabine farm,
where of course Horace may be as Epicurean as he pleases (as he
tells his fellow poet Tibullus in epistle 1.4), the idea, at first
uncomfortable, of the Stoic's absolutism and moral commitment
begins to come into its own. It's now a real and important question "whether Stertinius's insights were crazy," after all.

To Fuscus in epistle 1.10 Horace claims that, though his
friend may find the city's delights impossible to leave behind,
the Sabine farm is worth all of them to him. He is as disgusted
with his long over-indulgence in the city as a priest's runaway
slave is with eating the left-over wafercakes from sacrifices. The
mere scenery of the Sabine hills, and the comparison of the farm
with the grand villas around it, are beginning to suggest to him
the truth of the Stoic maxim "Live according to Nature." For
God is immanent in Nature as in man, and Nature is the book of
his will.

> If a man ought really to "live according to Nature,"
> he must find the ground to pitch his dwelling first:
> Can you show me a happier place than this rich
>   farmland?
> . . . .
> Does my grass smell worse than perfumed mosaic
>   pavements?   [*Epistles* 1.10.12–14, 18]

But Fuscus may still be happy and wise in his own way in
the city; Horace only wants him to visit the farm and argue the
point. This foreshadows the great opening lines of 1.16, which
will develop the theme of the Sabine farm as the ground of
ultimate self-realization to the highest pitch it achieves in the
book. But for the moment Horace's love of the country and
Fuscus's love of the city are just two views on the doxographical
page, alternate possibilities to be debated.

Horace writes in epistle 1.14 to his slave overseer on the
agellum, the little farm; as he pointedly calls it in the first line,
"the woods and small fields that give me back to myself." He
refuses the overseer's request to be sent back to Rome. The
overseer had asked for his job on the farm and is now bored

with it, in spite even of the company of the five respectable tenant farmers, who are leading citizens of the small town of Variae (modern Vicovaro) nearby. Horace claims he is only in Rome to console a friend in mourning for a recently deceased brother; his mind and spirit are already at the farm. Attempting to impress the slave, he deliberately forces his note and pushes his claims too far:

> You know my perfect consistency; how sadly I leave
> when my wretched business affairs call me to Rome.
> We do not admire the same things; that is the
>   difference
> between you and me. What you think is a wilderness
> of howling solitude, men like me call lovely, and
>   loathe
> your idea of delight: the brothels and greasy taverns.
>   [*Epistles* 1.14.16–21]

Horace claims to have acquiesced in the passage of time. He has given up the life of pleasure described in the *Epodes* and *Odes*, and is now eager only to till his own fields in quiet, enduring the laughter of his Sabine neighbors for his efforts at farming and building, in exchange for the envy and unpleasantness of society in the city. The tone is intentionally pompous and insincere. Obviously the reader is being set up for one more bout between Horace and his contradictory desires for luxury and for simplicity, before the sunburst of epistle 1.16. Even if they haven't overheard the dictation of relapses into complaint and confusion, slaves like Davus and the overseer must know a great deal more about Horace than is consistent with recognizing his "perfect consistency."

Epistle 1.15, of course, provides this contrast: the overseer of 1.14 might be imagined as justly furious if he read it. Horace's health, he says to his rich friend Numonius, requires a luxurious winter vacation that will make him young again and allow him to relapse into at least a version of the luxuries he tells the bailiff he has forsworn on account of age. His doctor (the emperor's own, Antonius Musa) has forbidden him Baiae, and (Horace says with complacency) that luxurious health resort is forced against its will to swallow the loss of his fashionable patronage and custom. He must therefore fall back on Velia or Salerno. So he asks Numonius to help him plan the trip, specifying that the miserable local wines of those towns, as commonplace as the wine he drinks at the farm, will not do for his pleasure trip. Horace needs to spend enough on the vacation to amuse and impress whatever woman he finds to sleep with there; and the food must be good enough to send him back as fat as a Phaeacian (the lazy people of the *Odyssey*, mentioned in epistle 1.2).

> You know that's me to the life: extolling what's
>   common
> and easy when money is low, and braving cheap fare;
> when luck comes and oils my wheels, I'm ready to
>   claim
> you rich folk alone are the Wise Men, live the good
>   life,
> with solid money displayed in your glittering villas.
>   [*Epistles* 1.15.42–47]

Again one sees that this relapse into hedonism is not a real conclusion but another introduction. But this time the greatest of the twenty poems, 1.16, is the result, and the rest are scaled gently down from it to the end. In its context, 1.15 says that Horace makes no claim that his pursuit of philosophy has made him an ascetic, that his surface appearance in society outside the Sabine farm is different from any other rich Roman's. But there is a core to his being that is not apparent when he is away at the edges of his travel map of Italy, or in the city, but does appear most clearly when he is at the center of all his places, the farm "that gives me back to myself," as he said in the first line of 1.14. Epistle 1.16 opens by describing it as it looks in summertime, impervious (as the countryside round Vicovaro is to this day) to the August heat lower down in Rome, and the symbol of the protection of Horace's inner self by philosophy and reflection from the hot strife and confusion of values in Rome. This is the implication of one of Horace's most shattering "conversational transitions," the transition from the description of the farm to the question of who Quinctius, Horace's rich young Roman addressee, really is, which explains itself easily. The farm is the

symbol of Horace's own personality at its most absolute and
independent pitch:

> You need not wonder, Quinctius, whether my farm
> feeds its master from the fields, or opulent olive
>   groves,
> of fruits and pastures and vines trained to the elms;
> I shall write you in full the form and lie of the
>   grounds.
> ....
> You would swear I had packed up Tarentum in flower
>   and brought it
> here. My fountain might give a river its name,
> since the Hebrus that waters Thrace is not purer nor
>   colder,
> the perfect cure for all headache and queasiness.
> This pleasant or, if you like, delightful retreat
> will give me back to you safe when September begins.
> *You* live well, if you take any care to be what we call
>   you,
> since all of us Romans call you a happy man.
> ....
> It is the shame of fools to hide festering sores
> untreated. If someone told of the wars you fought
> on land and sea, and flattered your idle ears with
> "Whether the people desires your well-being more,
> or you theirs, may Jupiter, Rome's guardian and your
>   own,
> keep ever debatable," you would know Augustus's
>   praise,
> not yours. When the people call you well schooled
>   and wise,
> can you answer by name to that description? Tell me.
> "But we both enjoy being called good men and wise."
> Who gives you this today can withdraw it tomorrow,
> just as if he makes a bad consul, he can unmake him.
> "Give me my fasces back." I give them and leave,
> unhappy. If he calls me thief and adulterer
> and shouts that I garrotted my own father,

> should I be stung by the lie and change my colors?
> False honors delight, and libel terrifies—what
> but the spoiled mind that needs teaching? Who is the
>   good man?
> "He keeps to our legal tradition, our laws and
>   precedents,
> he is trusted with many great cases for arbitration,
> his word and witness our juries take for pure truth."
> But his family and slaves and all his neighborhood
> know his inner meannesses, under the bright, fair
>   skin.   [*Epistles* 1.16.1–4, 11–18, 24–45]

Horace goes directly to the contrast between inner and outer man that the farm symbolizes by challenging Quinctius about what all Romans would ordinarily have taken to be a "good" man. A jurisconsult of reputation, whose word is as good as gold in court, was in fact the Roman upper-class ideal of a great and good man in peacetime. But even such a man might be wrong to believe his flatterers instead of his own inner voice. He would be no better, as the Stoics' favorite paradox went, than a slave after all. Second, Horace rather audaciously brings in Augustus and alludes to the aspects of his regime, even if they only affected the senatorial class and their equals, that were in fact tyrannical. A senator might already well tremble for his life to hear his military triumphs praised in the style now absolutely reserved to the imperial family. Even more daring is the hint that there is now a person (the people? Augustus?) who can take the fasces away even from consuls, and with impunity. Most audaciously of all, Horace makes out that the one limit to the imperial power is Stoic defiance: Even the emperor cannot order a good man to believe himself bad. The hints that Horace is thinking of the ability to survive not just Rome, but the imperial court itself, without moral damage come to fruition at the amazing end of the poem, when the implied Stoicism of its message is at last fully revealed in a moral allegory of Euripides' *Bacchae*. The final answer to the question "Who is the good man?" turns out to be this:

> The good man, the Wise Man, will dare to day,
>   "Pentheus,

guardian of Thebes, what can you compel me to bear
and endure, in my innocence?" "I must have all your
    goods."
"Flocks, property, furniture, silver, you mean: Take
    them."
"And confine you harshly, guarded, in handcuffs and
    chains."
"The God himself, when I wish, will set me free."
He means: I can die. Death is all things' finish-line.
                                      [*Epistles* 1.16.73–77]

This is one of the great moments in Horace. The sixteenth
epistle is the hexameter equivalent of the great "Tyrrhena
regum progenies" ode (3.29), and its thought shows the same
progression: the addressee in Rome, Horace on the Sabine farm;
Rome the home of merely external greatness that enslaves the
inner man, the Sabine farm capable of creating thoughts whose
greatness soars even to the abandonment of itself and of life.
The fusion of Plato, Euripides, Stoicism, and Horace's own
thought in these lines is unusually ambitious and exalted, mark-
ing a climax of the book. In the *Bacchae* Horace's allegory (perhaps drawing on lost Stoic allegories before him) makes Dionysus the character who symbolizes the Wise Man, because
the defiant young god incarnates the qualities the Stoics as-
cribed to their Wise Man, to the derision of the other philosophical schools. He alone is free, he alone is beautiful and desirable,
as well as good. By adding a line to Euripides' play that was not
there, Horace can mock the mere earthly king's notion that he
can take away another's "goods." That is only true to the extent
that the word means his "wealth." Pentheus is equally impotent
in threatening to imprison a spirit that can free itself from the
body by suicide in a moment. Moreover, if Horace is ever the
Roman Socrates, it is here: he is clearly thinking of Alcibiades'
contention in the *Symposium* that within Socrates' ugly, satyr-
like body was the image of the young Dionysus himself, and
claiming the same thing for the independent mind in his own
unimpressive, middle-aged body.

Most important of all, this is the passage in which he takes
on most directly, and I think resolves for the rest of his life and

work, the problem that Augustus the great authority figure posed for the first generation of his poets. Horace had chosen to support the regime, and he never went back on that. But he understood what the implications of absolute power were, even in the hands of a good emperor, and he could not honestly finish the subject of patronage and independence in *Epistles* 1 unless he touched somewhere the ultimate life-and-death questions that Augustus's version of autocracy brought up. Horace in this passage brings up deliberately and endorses the great Roman tradition, which he must have known was not over, of Republican suicides like Brutus's and Cato's in reply to absolutism. That may never be required of himself or any other particular person, but a human being without that resource in him has not arrived at self-knowledge, is not yet "good."

From this high vantage point Horace addresses epistles 1.17 and 1.18 to the evidently humble Scaeva and the much richer and more powerful Lollius, both starting careers in Rome, in the character of a client emeritus who has successfully climbed to what Disraeli called "the top of the greasy pole" and looks back with some cynicism on the means that got him there. Scaeva is advised that he still has time to withdraw to the country and live in obscurity, to "live unnoticed," if he likes his leisure and quiet, as the Epicureans recommended. Or if he likes he may flip down the page in his doxography to the opinions of the Hedonist Aristippus, who thought the advantages of paying court to the wealthy fully repaid the Wise Man's trouble. And Aristippus's arguments made sense as stated; Horace even carries them further: "It is not the lowest praise to have pleased great men; not every man can get to visit Corinth; men only give up because they fear they'll fail." But by the end of the exposition the whole moral has changed. The client starts out intending to be an honest man, but even his honesty is degraded into profit-seeking pretense by a system that can foul and degrade every good intention. Horace starts to advise that dignified silence will get a client more rewards than perpetual hints for gifts or complaints of poverty. But the moral he draws, as if he artfully fell back into suggesting the distastefulness of the whole process, is that "if the crow just feeds in silence, he gets much more food and much less fighting and envy." A client taken to

Brundisium (are we to think of the famous journey-satire?) or Sorrento who complains of the hard conditions of the journey is simply a whore complaining to get more money; his real troubles lose credence from his volubility about trivial ones, and they should. Such, Horace implies, are the unavoidable rules of patronage. Efforts to maintain one's dignity and independence can never be more than half-successes.

The same progression of thought underlies the epistle to Lollius: One can prepare oneself with all sorts of rationalizations for the life of a client, that one will be a true amicus and not a mere hanger-on and flatterer, that one will observe an Aristotelian mean between fulsomeness and unnecessary defiance. Still, it will be nothing if not galling to accept even the well-meant advice of a patron ("probably ten times worse a man than you are") and conform your expenses, your dress, your manners to what he considers your station. He is right, but the choice even of the good action is no longer your own. You may promise yourself to keep your mind steady with the help of books and what leisure you have. But in vain: you must lay aside your poetry with a good will and go out hunting with the patron whenever he chooses to hunt, and because he chooses. (Is Horace talking of Lollius or himself?) The only true recourse will be to study philosophy anyway in your few leisure hours, be careful of your inner integrity, and wait for the time when you can at last be independent and realize it in your own life:

> What makes you your *own* amicus?
> What gives you cleanness and balance: places and
>   profits,
> or a secret path, the way of the hidden life?
> When the cold Digentia makes me myself again,
> where Mandela's wrinkled, shivering peasants drink,
> what do you think I feel, my amicus, and pray?
> "Let me keep what I have now or less, and live to
>   myself
> what is left of my life, if the gods have indeed left
>   any;
> a year's good supply of books and of food laid in,

and no hanging in terror of what the next hour may
  bring.
It's enough to pray to Jove, who gives and can take
  away,
for life, for food; I will make my own peace of mind."
[*Epistles* 1.18.102–12]

Horace began epistle 1.17 by suggesting to Scaeva that the "hidden life" the Epicureans recommended was unambitious and unfulfilling; he concludes the pair of epistles in 1.18 by implying to Lollius that in some ways all the client's career gets you anyway, after wasting decades of your life on careful servilities, is back to the hidden life again. So in these final lines of 1.18 the themes of patronage, philosophy, place, aging, and reviewing one's life to find what one has gained rather than lost by being at an end point rather than a starting point, all harmoniously converge and complete themselves.

It remains only to discuss a fifth theme that has been quietly developing since the opening of the book: Maecenas is Horace's friend and the encourager and part-creator (for all the superficial complaints) of both his career and his poetry; for this book, like all Horace's others, manifests Horace's never-failing consciousness that he is writing poems and writing in a genre. Maecenas was given credit at the beginning for calling Horace back to poetry. The second poem analyzed poetry as philosophy. Various addressees throughout are poets as well as clients and patrons and fellow students of philosophy. In 1.18, not by accident, it is made a leading disadvantage of the clientela system that it makes demands on leisure that would better be spent on poetic composition as well as philosophy. The last two poems are devoted to bringing out and completing this theme; they review Horace's life from that standpoint to make a statement about his poetry. Horace addresses Maecenas again in 1.19 as one of his few intelligent critics, in a rather bitter little poem claiming that he is pleased neither with such superficial tributes of imitation he has so far received for the *Odes* and *Epodes*, nor with their failure so far to win the acclaim he hoped for. Because he has not condescended to advertise and recite them all over

Rome, he is accused óf complacently trusting in Maecenas's and Augustus's favor and caring nothing for his public. Since seven years later, in *Odes* 4, Horace says that "all the children of Rome, queen of cities, consent to give mé my place among the chorus of poets, and now I am no longer prey to the tooth of Envy" and that "I am pointed out by all that pass by as the true player of the Roman lyre" (4.3.12–16, 22–23), it must be a fact in some sense that the *Odes* and *Epodes* took years to be appreciated at their true value.

But that does not prevent Horace from sending his book of epistles out into the world in his epilogue, the twentieth and last poem, in a style as confident and grand as the *exegi monumentum* with which he concluded the *Odes*. (Indeed, the style is perhaps more grand because more subtle and humorous.) In 1.20 his book is addressed as a beautiful young slave eager for his freedom. More than that: he wants to exploit his beauty commercially and is eager to sell it to the public with the help of Horace's publishers and copiers, the Sosius brothers, who will polish him with pumice and offer him to all buyers. Well, the book will repent when his lovers tire of him, fold him up, and throw him aside. His popularity in Rome will last till he gets a little older and loses his novelty and the polish fades under his readers' pawing hands. Then he will have his choice of silently feeding moths or traveling out to the provinces, and his last fate will be to teach children in villages their lessons. Of course, this is nothing less than to claim that the book will be a classic and a schooltext all over the empire; and a tranquil splendor and pride comes over the closing lines as Horace tells the book what its lessons to the schoolchildren will forever be. The book will take Horace himself with it from time, from this very year, into timelessness. He joins a grand claim in the old-fashioned Republican tone that he had gained the approval of the city's greatest in peace and war, with a simpler personal characterization, which in the context of a book spent coming to terms with such patronage and the dangers it posed to his integrity and self-image, seems very pointed ("easy to anger and as easy to calm down").

> But when the warm evenings bring you more
> listeners,

you will tell them: A freedman's son, and born poor,
I spread wings broader and stronger than my nest,
so that what you detract from my birth adds to my
    merit.
The city's greatest approved me in peace and war;
I was short, and grey too soon, and liked the
    outdoors,
and was easy to anger and as easy to calm down.
And should any of them chance to ask my birthdate,
let him know I finished four times eleven Decembers
in the year that Lepidus and Lollius were consuls.

                                         [*Epistles* 1.20.19–28]

That is, 21 B.C., in December of which year his forty-fourth
birthday occurred. Roman letters were dated at the end; so is
Horace's epistle to his public, with the additional implication
that the year is, among other things, memorable forever for the
book. Unlike himself, the young book will grow old but not die.

Carmen saeculare *and* Odes 4

There is a little that can be known about Horace's life in the
period 20–13 B.C. Maecenas is no longer a force in the regime—
that apparently ended in the late twenties. There is one great
change in the first book of *Epistles:* Maecenas (significantly) no
longer feels the pressure of state business with which crowds
pester Horace in the streets, or which requires them to travel
together, or which needs to be got away from at any of Horace's
country places.

Maecenas's fall from favor was evidently only relative.
Above all, he wrote to Augustus from his deathbed in 8 B.C.,
having left all his immense property to the emperor: "Be as
mindful of Horatius Flaccus as if he were myself." The phrase
works two ways, surely: it expresses affection for Augustus as
sincerely as for Horace, or it means nothing—reluctant as we
are nowadays to admit that anybody personally cared for the
Princeps! But if Maecenas's credit and friendship with the emperor partly survived, we also know that Augustus successfully
insisted on replacing Maecenas as the chief patron and ad-

dressee of Horace's poetry, sometime in the years after the first book of *Epistles*. He also made every effort, though with less success, to make Horace leave Maecenas's circle and join his own. He first offered an official position in his suite to Horace and then tried to make him a regular attendant of the new court on a less formal basis. We know from Suetonius's life of Horace that neither offer was accepted.

But if Horace refused Augustus's offers of personal friendship, he was not unwilling to find another way. He had accepted obligations from the emperor, including two "large gifts" Suetonius mentions. By the end of his life Horace owned a house in Tibur itself, which may have been one of them, but it is amazing that Horace published not a word of poetic thanks for either largesse. He had also been given something else, in the commission to write and perform the *Carmen saeculare*, the *Centennial Hymn*, at Augustus's great Ludi Saeculares or Centennial Games of 17 B.C., for which he was not merely formally grateful. The suggestion of tension in Suetonius's story has to be reconciled with Horace's clear and unambiguous delight in one thing he got from Augustus's patronage: the dizzy glory of standing for a moment at the summit of all things Roman when he directed the singing of his hymn at the Centennial Games. He was given for once the opportunity to be a Roman Pindar, paid to celebrate the glory of his patron in poetry performed to the accompaniment of music and choruses and literally before the whole Roman public, even in that urbanized and sophisticated society. One risks storytelling on inadequate evidence here. But not that much. The *Carmen saeculare*, a prayer to Apollo and Diana for the prosperity of the Roman state, bears signs of including items that Augustus personally suggested as patron. Its stanzas on family life are duly there, and are not as crude an effort as those in the Roman Odes. The train of thought is less forced: The poem asks the gods to prosper the decrees of the senate on family life, so that a future generation of Romans may appear in equally great numbers to celebrate the next centennial. In the ancient world depopulation was a real fear.

Similarly, the poem's warlike tone is much diminished from that of the Roman Odes: it celebrates peace, the mercy that Augustus has shown the defeated, and the respect that he has

won from Rome's enemies across the frontiers of the wide
empire.

> Grant his wishes, who gives these white cattle;
> he is the son of Venus and Anchises,
> his wars are always victories, he is gentle
>   to the defeated!
> For now the Medes are yielding to Roman power,
> the Alban fasces respected on land and sea;
> Scythians, once proud, and even India,
>   seek his counsel.
>
> [*Carmen saeculare* 49–56]

This will also be the theme for all Horace's state odes in the
fourth book: the Augustan Peace and the happiness of Italy, war
and violence pushed back hundreds of miles (as by Tiberius and
Drusus) to unheard-of frontiers.

The *Carmen saeculare*, like all the great state odes, is difficult
to categorize in modern Western terms, because it is an unambiguous and unironic praise of social order. But there are other
theories of poetry that might suit it and them. It could be seen,
for example, as a fine poem in what the seventeenth-century
Japanese Noh dramatist Zeami called the lowest of the five
genres of poetry: the celebration of order on earth.* The next
three of the five genres embody ascending intensities of what
Zeami called *yugen*, the dyeing of the thread from which the
poem is woven with the colors of human feeling, in ascending
ranks of intensity from the most earthbound to the most spiritual. The fifth and highest involves the sublimity in which old
age transcends every beauty of youth and the spring with a new
beauty of its own, and few critics would think that a poor definition to apply to the greatest of Horace's last personal lyrics in
book 4. The lowest genre, that of "celebration" of the order of
the universe ruled by heaven, should precisely *not* be dyed with
deep human feelings, and is exemplified by the classic poem:

> May our august Emperor
> Live for thousands of years

---

*There is a fascinating account of his system in Makoto Ueda, *Zeami, Basho,
Yeats, Pound: A Study in Japanese and English Poetics* (London, 1965), pp. 19–25.

Like a venerable pine tree,
So that we may all live
Peacefully under his shade.

"There is order in the universe," Ueda comments, "ruled by heaven; there is order in the nation ruled by the Emperor; man, in this world, wants to live for as long as he can. The audience will feel joy and happiness as he sees this type of play enacted."

I somehow find in this definition the perfect way to view the *Carmen saeculare* and the tributes in *Odes* 4 to Augustus and the Augustan Peace. The Romans of the empire were as sincere as the Japanese of classical times in admiring this genre of imperial ritual and worship and this genre of literature and art, understanding nonetheless that the possibilities of poetry and drama only began there. What Horace celebrates in these late odes, after all, as the Roman Odes of 23 B.C. could not yet, was the massive descent of what was to be 250 years of virtually unbroken peace, on Italy, Greece, and all the interior provinces of the Roman Empire. Perhaps he would look a fool if history had gone differently, but his instinct was proved right by the event. And he celebrated this vision of peace when it was not yet familiar to the propaganda and ideology of the empire, but still immediate and new.

Book 4 of the *Odes* combines a number of stately and formal poems on the triumphs of Augustus and the empire, and on the immortality and power of poetry as exemplified in Horace's own work. The combination lifts the state poetry a little above the purely worldly, formal, and celebratory mode Zeami describes into the realm of self-conscious irony, for the tendency of the poems-on-poetry is to remind addressee and reader that all happy worlds and heroic deeds, even all gods, are the creation of the singer who sings them. In addition, there are a number of personal poems that dwell on the passage of time, aging, the fading of love, the undiminished authority of death. In Zeami's terms these would be the poems of yugen, dyed with the human feelings the state poems lack. Read in sequence with the others, they make a statement that any intelligent citizen of the empire could decipher, about the limitations even of golden ages of human "happiness." A hundred years later, when the imagery of the imperial peace was so familiar and its achievements so real that even the most disdainful Stoic could speak of it with respect, Epictetus put the same thought this way: No Stoic cosmopolis on earth, if that is what the empire is, can by itself save a man from the futility of desire, from pain, death and ultimate things.

> For look: Caesar appears to offer us perfect peace, because there are no wars, no battles, no brigandage or piracies of importance, but at all hours any of us may travel or sail, from the East where the sun rises to the West where it sets. Does that mean he can give us peace from fever and shipwreck, from fire, earthquake, and lightning? From sexual desire? Certainly not. From sorrow and envy? Certainly not. But the doctrine of philosophers promises us peace from these things also.
>
> [Arrian *Discourses* 3.13.9–10]

The doctrine of poets also deals honestly with such limitations. Horace opens *Odes* 4 with a personal poem that has hidden behind it a similar structure of thought—though as becomes a poet, not a philosopher, he makes clear in it that he does not want to be "saved" from the pain of sexual desire, nor give in all that gracefully to aging and the imminence of death. But it seems also that he at last deals more honestly with Augustus's moral legislation. The peaceful and prosperous Italy that Augustus is creating either has a place for bachelors like Horace and their male and female lovers, good citizens all, beside the respectable married people, or Horace's book itself will make no sense. The fourth book of *Odes* is indeed a kind of Augusteum or temple to the imperial order and the imperial peace, such as were soon to be erected in provincial cities all over the empire. But it is a sophisticated Augusteum, one that praises the emperor's rule over all he can reasonably be supposed to rule, yet concedes him in the end no domination over the world of human love and desire, whatever his efforts at moral legislation. Not does Horace grant Augustus, for all his great building projects, any victory over the relentless passage of time and the transience of human life, except the victory only the poet can create, by enshrining a ruler on the same terms as himself in his works of art. There is a translation of 4.1 by Ben Jonson that (in modern spelling) is as readable as any modern one, and my quotations are from that:

> Venus, again thou mov'st a war
> Long intermitted. Pray thee, pray thee, spare;
> I am not such, as in the reign
> Of the good Cynara I was; refrain,
> Sour mother of sweet Loves,* forbear
> To bend a man now at his fiftieth year,
> Too stubborn for commands so slack;
> Go where youth's soft entreaties call thee back.
> More timely hie thee to the house,
> With thy bright swans, of Paullus Maximus;
> There jest, and feast, make him thine host,
> If a fit liver thou dost seek to toast;†
> For he's both noble, lovely, young,
> And for the troubled client files his tongue,
> Child of a hundred arts, and far
> Will he display the ensigns of thy war.

Venus, the goddess of the imperial house, urges Horace into war/love/poetry again after a long interval; but he refers her instead to a young man whose qualifications of patrician birth and legal learning are not those of a lover but a good Roman husband; Paullus Fabius Maximus was at this time soon to be married to Augustus's cousin. In thanks for his marriage, Maximus will adopt the imperial family's official habit of temple building and erect to Venus a shrine where

> twice a day in sacred lays
> The youths and tender maids shall sing thy praise,
> And in the Salian manner meet
> Thrice 'bout thy altar with their Ivory feet.

---

*Literally, "cruel mother of Cupids," but Jonson points the antithesis still more sharply.

†Since the liver in antiquity was considered the seat of the emotions.

Horace's worship of Venus is different:

> Me now nor wench nor wanton boy
> Delights, nor credulous hope of mutual joy,
> Nor care I now healths to propound,
> Or with fresh flowers to girt my temple round.

This is very much like what Horace told the farm bailiff in
Epistles 1.14: "not ashamed I had fun, but ashamed not to quit it
now." But the capacity for lyric poetry is the capacity to love and
dream, even against age and hope, and Horace's thoughts are
still with the beautiful wrestlers and swimmers on the Campus
Martius. Only this time the beautiful boy is given not a Greek
but an Italian name, Ligurinus; he and Horace are both Romans
of the new empire:

> But why, oh why, my Ligurine,
> Flow my thin tears down these pale cheeks of mine?
> Or why, my well-graced words among,
> With an uncomely silence fails my tongue?
> Hard-hearted, I dream every night
> I hold thee fast! but fled hence, with the light,
> Whether in Mars his field thou be
> Or Tiber's winding stream, I follow thee.

Literally: "Now in my dreams at night I hold you captured;
now follow you as you speed across the lawn of the Campus
Martius, (follow) you through the flowing waters, hard-hearted
one." Jonson saw correctly that this says with ambiguous syntax
that Horace watched Ligurinus run and swim both in his
dreams and in reality; and all but exceeded the grammatical
capacities of English in (successfully) reproducing the ambiguity
of dream and reality in his version. Every reader sees the pathos
of the contrast: the handsome young patrician about to be
adopted by marriage into the imperial family, the old poet
wavering between resignation to his own loneliness and the
hope of one more brief dream—that of love. In the context of the
book, Horace also quietly and firmly makes them both equally
legitimate worshippers of the imperial family goddess, Venus,
both equally legitimate beneficiaries of the Augustan Peace.

All the other poems of the first pentad of the fifteen are "about" poetry and the state. Ode 4.2 is to an addressee symbolic of reconciliation, Mark Antony's son Iullus Antonius, brought up by Octavia after Antony's death, and now in Augustus's high favor. Iullus Antonius wrote poetry himself. Horace addresses him as they wait for the celebrations that attend Augustus's return in 13 B.C. from several years in Gaul, founding Roman cities and supervising with Tiberius and Drusus the first stages of his greatest military project in the West: that of extending the frontier of the empire hundreds of miles north to the Danube and the Rhine, and if possible the Elbe, and thus securing for generations the peace of the interior provinces.

The greatness of Pindar is inimitable, Horace tells Antonius at the opening (as Cowley's paraphrase has it, "The Phoenix Pindar is a vast species alone"):

> Whoever will have his poems vie with Pindar's,
> Iullus, struggles with feathers glued with wax
> by Daedalus's art; gives a name to the clear
> sea that he falls in.   [*Odes* 4.2.1–4]

But in fact, in 1.3 Horace celebrates the growing fame of his odes as if he were himself a Roman Pindar, and in 1.4 he ventures on a celebration of immense mock-Pindaric grandeur of Tiberius's and Drusus's conquests in the North.

The fourth ode is an immense double panel of grand periodic verse like 3.4, but with an easier logical connection between its halves. The conquest of Switzerland and south Germany by Tiberius and Drusus in 15 B.C. had added more space to the Roman Empire relative to the loss of blood than any Roman conquest in history; the young princes had been given more an exercise in space and logistics, and a venture into the unknown, than a war assignment. The Rhaeti and Vindelici and the other tribes of the new province had been able to put up just enough resistance to qualify the campaign as a campaign; the princes were far short of the decisive battle that a triumph required. The first part of Horace's ode is all fire and air as he conveys his delight at the ease with which the frontiers of war have been lifted hundreds of miles north from peaceful Italy. In a long-breathed period of humorous, self-conscious grandeur, he compares the young princes to eaglets and lion cubs that are true scions of a family of eagles and lions. Their first efforts at war have conquered peoples so unheard-of that their ways are not even yet to be read of in the imperial libraries, and the poet must throw up his hands and wait for enlightenment later.

> As an eagle, born the minister of lightning,
> whom the king of gods made king of wandering
>   birds,
> Jupiter, who found him faithful
> raping blond Ganymede to heaven,
> when youth and inherited vigor drive him
> from his nest, still ignorant what to do,
> now the spring clouds are pushed away
> and winds first teach him clumsy flight,
> trembling; soon among timid sheepfolds
> life and energy send him warring,
> next even against struggling serpents
> his love of war and feasting drives him;
> as baby roe-deer in the rich meadows
> see a young lion, newly weaned,
> fresh from his tawny mother's udder,
> death waiting in his sharp young teeth:
> so Rhaetians warring in mountain-shadow
> and Vindelici saw young Drusus . . . .   [*Odes* 4.4.1–18]

It is because he is celebrating a victory over logistic difficulties and empty spaces rather than enemies that Horace can convey the joy and ease of it simply by suspending this long, almost parodically exaggerated period in air till it comes to ground at a halfway point on the honoree's name. (It goes on for ten more lines and comes to a full stop at last on the mention of Augustus and both brothers.) The name in turn generates a thought. Pindar's theme of inborn nobility in his victors can be revived in Roman terms, for Tiberius and Drusus are descended from the Claudius Nero, who turned the course of the Second Punic War in Rome's favor at the Metaurus in 207 B.C., where Hannibal's brother Hasdrubal was killed and his head taken to south Italy and thrown into Hannibal's camp. They are cubs of a great house of the ancient Republic, as well as Augustus's stepsons, and both traditions are incarnate in them.

The theme of space can be used to remind the reader that not two hundred years earlier Rome itself had seen the enemy ride up to its walls. Hannibal roved Italy till a Claudius stopped him; now the young Claudii roam lands hardly known. This theme is treated more seriously, but the humor remains. Hannibal is represented, with a cheerful disdain for realism, as reacting to the news of his brother's death by bursting out in uncontrollable admiration for Rome, and that in a string of Pindaric and even Vergilian similes. The state poetry of book 4 draws on the *Aeneid*; and Hannibal is represented as knowing not only the legend of Aeneas but the very simile in which Vergil compared Aeneas, in his anguished resistance to Carthaginian Dido's complaints, to a deep-rooted tree (*Aeneid* 4.441–49).

> "Stags that fall to hungry wolves,
> we are hunted now, and our best triumph
> is to evade and hide. This nation—
> which came forth stronger from burning Troy,
> whose sacred objects, tossed on the Tuscan sea,
> whose children and whose aged wise men
> came safe to these Ausonian lands—
> is an oak, though pruned by double axes,
> that keeps on leafing on black Algidus.
> Though hacked and shorn of limbs, it gathers
> spirit and strength to math the steel:
> or a Hydra, taking strength from its wounds,
> growing again, defying Hercules . . . ."
>
> [*Odes* 4.4.50–62]

The poem has already turned into a song of victory and peace, not warfare, and the pentad is concluded with ode 4.5. This is a poem put in the mouth of the Roman plebs, who fulsomely praise Augustus's achievement of peace and prosperity, long anxiously for his coming return, and rejoice (dutifully) in the improvement of their morals, and the tranquility and freedom with which they can praise him, first sober and then filled with wine, on their holidays. Odes 4.4 and 4.5 will find their mirror in the two connected odes that end the book,

4.14 on the pacification of the world by Augustus in war, and 4.15 on what Horace declares is the far greater achievement: the peace and prosperity of Italy and its people.

But with ode 4.6 Horace begins a second pentad that fulfills the promise of 4.1 by being more colored with personal emotion in its statements. The themes of space and peace in 4.4 and 4.5, so suitable to the praises of the imperial order, begin to be undercut by the theme of time and its passage. This theme is already present in ode 4.4, with its comparison of Rome's empire today with Rome in the times of Hannibal, and in ode 4.5, with its evocation of the primitive Golden Age. If the *Carmen saeculare* did not call forth from Horace anything like the color of personal emotion in its composing, the experience of the performance itself did, to judge from the imaginary prologue that he later added to it as ode 4.6. The Great Patron could after all create for Horace an undreamed-of experience that even Maecenas could not: standing in public with his lyre before a choir of the children of all the most ancient families of Rome, at the center of what Augustus intended should be a festival that would dwarf all previous magnificence in the giving of Roman festivals.

Horace invokes Apollo as the patron of Roman history. Apollo mercilessly stuck down the arrogance of Niobe, and of Achilles, who if he had lived would have burnt the children of Troy alive in their mothers' wombs. Prophetically, he rejected and destroyed the hero of Homeric violence and warfare, and chose instead to aid and preserve Aeneas in his escape from Troy, to begin the long process that built the empire and the imperial peace. Apollo is the patron also of Horace—to whom he gave "the spirit of poetry and the name of poet"—and of the centennial song and its chorus. But in a splendid concluding turn, Horace in the true Pindaric spirit remembers that in this immense wheel of generations the present moment of glory is turning and passing away into history, will last only as long as the hymn itself, and that another turn of the wheel will make the poet only a name to another generation:

> Unmarried girls of rank, noble children
> of noble fathers,

watched over always by the great Diana,
who governs deer and lynxes with her bow,
keep to the Sapphic meter and the accents
    struck by my fingers,
singing rightly Apollo, son of Leto,
rightly the moon goddess, waxing above us,
who forwards the harvest and swiftly rolls
    the headlong months by:
Married soon, you will say, "I bless the gods
that when the turning years brought the festival
I recited the hymn; I learned the verses
    of the poet Horace."   [*Odes* 4.6.31–44]

Read rightly, then, this sudden invocation of passing time,
this audacious leaving of his name to echo at the end, a memory
when he is gone, is Horace's perfect introduction to the two
central poems of the book, 4.7 and 4.8. It brings up the thought
that no matter how much a human society mirrors the order of
heaven, mankind is the tragic prisoner of time. In 4.7, death is
the fate of all mortals; in 4.8 the poet's gift to heroes and em-
perors is more precious than any riches because without it their
deeds would not even be remembered as what they are—or
rather, as what he chooses to call them.

In 4.7 Horace addresses a nobleman learned in the law, like
Maximus. The imagery is like that of ode 1.4: spring brings the
thought of death, but the examples (suitably to the book's
theme) now include Aeneas, founder of Rome, and Theseus,
the older lover, trying to free his own Ligurinus from death.

Now the snow has escaped in all directions,
    grass returns to flatland, wreaths to trees,
Earth turns changes, and streams sink, back to size,
    into their pleated ways.
With nymphs and her twins, the Grace again dares
    lead the dance naked . . . No, no hope
of no dying: that is the year's round warning,
    and the hour's which tears
the teat of the morning away.
. . . .
New moons are quick to make good the losses

of the night sky; but when we sink
where Aeneas the good and wealthy Tullus
sank, we are dust and shade.
. . . .
When you do die, and are made the subject
of a classic judgment, dear friend,
no influence, no brilliant pleas, no goodness
will gain a release for you:
Diana does not free Hippolytus,
so pure, from the shadows under us,
nor can Theseus tear the chains from his
precious Pirithous.
[*Odes* 4.7.1–9, 13–16, 21–28; Richard Emil Braun translation]

Even this great poem, then, gains something from being
considered in the context of its book; and the poem-on-poetry
that follows it gains much more, for its real subject is not its
addressee, Censorinus, but the whole cycle of Horace's praise-
poems, particularly those to Augustus.

I would give bright cups of Corinthian bronze,
Censorinus, to all my friends; I would give
bronze tripods, ancient prizes of brave Greeks,
and you would not receive the least dear.
. . . .
But that's not in my power, nor is your estate
nor yet your soul greedy for such delights;
you love poems, and poems are what I can
give, knowing the value of the gift.
. . . .
If there were no words for the good things you did,
there would be no reward. What would the son
of Mars and Ilia be if a dead silence
mocked and destroyed the merits of Romulus?
. . . .
Heaven is the muse's gift, it is by her means
Hercules takes his longed-for place at the banquets
of Jove; and Castor and Pollux, stars in heaven,
snatch the wave-beaten ships from the abyss;

and Dionysus, adorned by her with vine-leaves,
receives our prayers and brings them to good ˉissue.

[*Odes* 4.8.1–4, 9–12, 21–24, 29–34]

This is strong language: not just the deified princes and
heroes but the gods themselves are in a sense mere talk, a language of poets that creates the reality it does not find. All the
great classic poets, Horace among them, are vividly aware of the
gap between the artificial loyalties and enthusiasms of religion
and the state, and the inadequate language of art that supports
them, and behind that the tragic unintelligibility of nature, time,
and death. The "frightful realism," *fürchtbare Realität*, that
Goethe surprised his friends by attributing to Horace's ornate
lyrics, appears nowhere more than in these two great centerpieces.

The ninth ode honors one of Augustus's generals who had
lost a whole legion to the Sygambri in 17 B.C.; he was allowed to
redeem his reputation by participating in their ultimate defeat.
The message conveyed is that the emperor, through his poet,
honors his defeated but brave generals as well as the victorious
princes of the imperial house. It admonishes Lollius at length
that "brave men lived before Agamemnon," but perished un-
wept and unhonored because they lacked their poet. The moral
of ode 4.8 is reinforced: poetry creates reputation, from whatever material is given it, victory or defeat. On this basis the
poem goes on as much to instruct Lollius in, as to ascribe to him,
the qualities of the wise man who soars above time and circum-
stance and disappointment, and fears disgrace but not death.
The tenth ode, appropriately, concludes this pentad of reflections on the swift passage of time, on death, and on the "immortality" of poetry and the ambiguous relation of its language
to reality, by representing even the beauty of the young
Ligurinus as brief and powerless before the swiftness of time.

You who can still use Venus's gifts with such cruelty
and power: when rough hairs surprise your pride
and the locks that flutter over your shoulders fall
and the skin that makes the brightness of roses pale
changes and covers with hair Ligurinus's face,

you will often lament to the different you in your
    mirror
and say: what I feel now, why could that boy not feel,
or that perfect face return and match my new spirit?
                                                    [*Odes* 4.10]

A poet of bisexuality, arranging his book round themes of
time, might be expected to save the presentation of his relationship to his women and his friends for last, as going so much
deeper into the passage of time; and that is in fact what happens
in the third and last pentad of book 4. Ode 4.11 invites Phyllis, a
fellow musician who is getting on in years like Horace himself,
to (apparently) the Sabine hills to drink and sing and stay with
him in spring. The poem would thus reproduce the same scenario and imagery as 1.17 and 3.28, if it were not for a new
theme: Phyllis and Horace share the disappointments of age.
Ode 4.11 makes amends for the tone of the earlier Old-Woman-
as-Lecher poems. In its beautiful last stanzas the notion at last
appears that one looked for in vain in the earlier poems: that an
older woman can suffer unrequited love for a young man without being a scarecrow or an object of ridicule; in fact, she resembles Horace himself. It is the ides of April, "the day from which
my own Maecenas numbers his gathering years." Maecenas, if
no longer Horace's principal public patron, is here reaffirmed as
part of the poet's private world, growing older birthday by
birthday. With this suggestion of the sacredness of friendship
and the unavoidable passage of time, Horace turns in a friendly
spirit to address Phyllis's disappointment in her young lover.
Just as he had amused himself by putting a string of ambitious
similes in the defeated Hannibal's mouth, he first tries to laugh
away Phyllis's pain with grand mythological comparisons that
satirize her ambition in picking such a person to fall in love with.
But then Horace changes the tone at the end to complete, affectionate seriousness:

You are in love with Telephus. He is young,
and a young girl whose life is not like yours,
but rich and wild, has beaten you, keeps him in
    chains

> he is happy to wear.
> Poor scorched Phaethon's story should deter
> your grasping hopes; another grave example,
> Pegasus, who spurned his earthbound rider
>   Bellerophontes,
> warns you: Find yourself lovers who make better
> pairs, reason your way past the sin of hoping
> where there is no hope, shun your unequals; come,
>   last of my loves,
> I will never warm to a woman after you;
> learn with me verses for that enchanting
> voice of yours to sing me. Music lightens
>   our black depressions.   [*Odes* 4.11.21–36]

In 4.13, the last of the Old Woman poems, Horace brings this series to a more harmonious close. Lyce, like the other repulsive old women, wants young lovers she cannot have. But here too Horace admits some sympathy with her amid the mockery. He loved her once, she was once as beautiful as anyone he ever loved except Cinara, and the pain that Lyce's foolishness and lost beauty cause him is pain for his own lost youth.

> Where's the compelling attraction, the bright skin,
> the limber walk; what is there left of her,
> of her who breathed loves,
> who stole me from myself . . . ?
> . . . .
>   The fates that assigned so little
> time to Cinara saved
> for Lyce all the years of the female crow,
> only so that the fiery young could glance,
> not without gales of laughter,
> at a poor old torch in ashes.   [*Odes* 4.13.17–20, 23–28]

On this new note of mockery of the Old-Woman-as-Lecher, with sympathy and fellow-feeling at last mixed in, Horace leaves the theme of lovers and old age. The book concludes with two odes celebrating Augustus's happy return. In 4.14, the Senate and people are said equally to wonder what honors and titles

can further adorn Augustus, now the greatest prince in the
world, his greatness augmented most recently by the victories of
Tiberius and Drusus in Rhaetia. But the real theme of the poem
is Augustus's unbroken success in campaign after campaign in
achieving peace. The great map of the empire, so often a theme
in the lyrics, makes one last magnificent appearance to under-
line that the glory of warfare is peace:

> For since the day
> when Alexandria knelt before you
> opening her harbors and empty palace,
> for fifteen years and more your Fortune
> has brought your wars the right conclusion.
> . . . .
> Before you Spaniards who never yielded,
> Medes and Indians, nomad Scythians
> stand awed, silent, true protector
> of Italy and her mistress, Rome;
> and she whose fountains still are veiled,
> the Nile; the Ister, hurrying Tigris,
> the Ocean whose unheard of monsters
> bay at the farthest shores of Britain,
> the Gauls who never shrank from death,
> the harsh Iberian province listen;
> Sygambri, that rejoiced in murder,
> put down their weapons in veneration.
>   [*Odes* 4.14.34–38, 41–52]

In the real world, one has to admit, Augustus's commands
did not as yet carry all that loudly and clearly to such distant
lands. But Horace does not deserve to be laughed at for that; he
is conveying a great vision, the vision for which Rome most
deserves to be remembered, which Augustus had now brought
considerably further than the horizon: that of a world, the whole
Mediterranean world, at peace with itself and respected by its
neighbors. Ode 4.14 and the great concluding poem, 4.15, are
thus a pair: The peace around the edges of the imperial map
only waits to be sung by its first and principal beneficiaries, the
Italians, for the song to conclude. Horace conjures up a picture
of them at peace, singing of "Troy, Anchises, and the offspring

of fostering Venus," which fuses the notions "singing of Augustus" (Venus's descendant), "singing the *Aeneid*" (whose hero is Venus's son), "singing of our origins," and "singing of the creative power of love" into one simple light that brilliantly concludes and unites the whole book. And his problem with the moral legislation is over. Having made himself, Ligurinus, Phyllis, and Lyce perfectly plausible Romans, free to work out their brief lives as they like under the new peace, he can say without any further irony that "we, our wives and children" (ours, in the sense that any single person might say "our children" in talking of her or his country as a whole) will join the song:

> Apollo, when I would sing of battles
> and conquered cities, rang on the strings, warning
> not to sail out on the Etruscan sea
> in such small craft. Caesar, your reign
> has brought rich harvests back to our fields
> and brought the eagles back to Jupiter,
> forced back at last from the lofty Parthian
> temples, and, since there is no warfare,
> closed Janus's doors,* and pulled the reins
> tight on all licentious wandering
> from the true order; exiled crime;
> brought back the ancient art and training
> by which the name of Rome, the power
> of Italy once grew great; the greatness
> and fame of the empire now spreads out
> from the evening to the rising sun.
> . . . .
> And we on festival days and workdays,
> with Dionysus's happy gifts
> before us, and our wives and children,
> with solemn prayers to the gods as prelude,
> will sing to the Lydian pipes our song
> of princes' work done in our ancient

*The temple of Janus was closed when Rome was not at war; Augustus closed it for the first time in hundreds of years.

fathers' manner; Troy and Anchises,
and his offspring though beneficent Venus.

[*Odes* 4.15.1–16, 25–32]

So the last words of the last ode recur to the first words of the first ode, and as goddess of love the imperial family goddess binds public and private poetry together into one. Horace's state poetry tends in many modern studies to be dismissed as mere grandiose rhetoric, in sharp and unreconciled contrast to the real poetry of the "personal" poems, and there is no doubt that this contrast exists in his earlier lyrics and is sometimes merely jarring. But the fourth book of odes, his farewell to lyric poetry, is an immense and successful effort not just to place the two worlds side by side but to make them cohere: he reconciles the world in which death, the passage of time, the transience of love and youth have complete and ultimate power over the individual, with the world in which it is possible to join in and celebrate the community, its history, and its triumphs, its hopes for as long and peaceful a life as the world allows.

Epistles 2

After the publication of *Odes* 4, Horace may have ceased to write. He died on November 27, 8 B.C., shortly after Maecenas's death in the same year. So his promise in *Odes* 2.17 to accompany Maecenas on every road, even the last, came true; whether from grief or by coincidence, there is no evidence. One thing about his death sounds strange for a Roman who figured in business and society as importantly as Horace did. Death came to him suddenly, Suetonius claims, so suddenly that he only had time to summon witnesses and dismiss his property into Augustus's hands. Augustus is known from other sources to have been a careful administrator of estates left to him, and Horace could well have trusted him to distribute any secondary bequests that he had promised to friends and to free slaves who had been promised their freedom. Such "nuncupatory" or declaratory wills were legal by Roman law as they are in ours, if reduced to writing as soon as possible after death and subscribed by the witnesses. But Romans of rank customarily made their wills into lengthy farewell-card lists of friends and favored acquaintances, using small bequests and namings to residuary legacies in the second and third degree to make sure every amicus received his due mention. That elaborate form of Roman politeness the poet dispensed with. It was unusual behavior; Horace's will is apparently the only recorded example in Roman history of a declaratory will, legal though they were. Was the Horace of real life so withdrawn from everyone in his last years except Maecenas that he disdained this social gesture? Or so involved with life that he regarded the writing of a will at all with distaste? Like much of our limited knowledge about the historical Horace, this story leaves us uncertain.

One or other of the three poems in the so-called second book of *Epistles* may belong to this late period, but modern scholarship tends to hold that they belong rather to the period 20–12 B.C. At various times after the publication of the first book of *Epistles* Horace added three longer poems to the collection that make a second "book": an epistle to Augustus (2.1), another (2.2) to the Florus who was the addressee of *Epistles* 1.3, and a treatise on the art of poetry (2.3) addressed to a Calpurnius Piso and his two sons, the polite fiction being that the sons are young poets of promise who need Horace's advice. The date of *The Art of Poetry* is so uncertain that it may even have been written before *Epistles* 1, in the late 20s. The dates of their composition may perhaps have come in the reverse of their conventional order, 3–2–1, with *The Art of Poetry* the earliest, the epistle to Florus second (not very long after *Epistles* 1). The epistle to Augustus would then come last, after 17 B.C. and perhaps even just after *Odes* 4: it refers to the *Carmen saeculare*, and Suetonius says it was provoked by Augustus's desire to have at least one of Horace's hexameter poems, not just his lyric poems, addressed to himself.

The three poems have many themes in common, because they are all three "Artes poeticae" of a kind. *The Art of Poetry* offers instruction to a younger generation of poets, symbolized by the Pisones. They are to continue further—for example, by the conquest of the tragic and comic genres—the triumphs already won by the poets of Horace's time in creating a more sophisticated kind of poetry and literature than the Republic had known. The epistle to Augustus considers the progress of Roman poetry and literature from the point of view of the emperor's duty to help in this process. Augustus's successful fostering of the kind of writing that Vergil, Varius, and Horace have done for him already should be continued to a new generation of poets whom Horace hopes he will encourage to be equally creative, subtle, and free. The epistle to Florus integrates some great statements of Horace's arduous personal ideals as a poet with a more complete and explicit life-review. Horace works his way, through powerful images of death and resignation, to a positive statement of a new life and a new kind of poetry. The great subjects of his earlier lyrics are like a banquet to be left to the young; Horace himself is on a new quest both in life and in art.

Horace treats thoughts throughout his work like pieces in a mosaic, to be transformed by rewriting and replacement and a different context. He is never ashamed to repeat them in varied form. And thus many a topic reappears in all three epistles, stated variously to suit the three themes: poetry from the point of view of pure art; from that of Augustus, the state, and society; and considered as part of a personal statement about Horace himself. All three poems stress in impressive passages the importance and dignity of the poet's role in Roman society, contrasting them with the low, acquisitive ideals of Roman business life that distract Romans from valuing the contribution of the arts. In the epistle to Augustus Horace tells the emperor that though poets look too unsoldierly and too unconcerned with property to be good Romans, they are in fact among the best, and he pointedly cites his own *Carmen saeculare* as the climactic example. If Augustus believes it was any use to propitiate the gods and ask them through Horace's chorus for peace and good harvest, Horace implies, he has already tacitly assented to the highest old-fashioned view of the sacred character of poetry and its necessity to the state (*Epistles* 2.1.102–38).

The epistle to Florus pictures the work of the poet, dazzlingly, as combining the spirit of a Roman censor, with authority to expel without mercy or protect and naturalize any word in the Roman language, with the arduous physical labors of a ballet dancer: the true poet thus works twice as hard as even the highest-ranking senatorial magistrate (2.2.109–25). *The Art of Poetry* tells the Pisones that if the Greeks were truer poets than any Romans yet, it is because they were not corrupted by the concentration on account books and splitting pennies into farthings that characterizes Roman business education (2.3.323–32). Horace reminds them, both ironically and seriously, that the true value of poetry is such as to make the truths symbolized in the ancient Greek legends about the lyres of Orpheus, Amphion, and Apollo as real now as ever (lines 391–408).

All three poems teach throughout that in so advanced and sophisticated a society as Rome's, the spirit of the great ancient Greeks, by whatever process of free inspiration Homer and Pindar and the tragic poets achieved their results, can be brought over only at the price of endless labor in the spirit of Callimachus and the Alexandrians. Study, sleepless labor, and above all submission to the real pain, indignity, and disappointment of cancellation, revision, acceptance of criticism from the qualified, and revision again, are recommended over and over. The result should be a style so perfect and so apparently simple that the labor that went into its making is invisible until those who think it really simple try to imitate it. In *The Art of Poetry* this is the poet's chief task, and the Pisones are reminded pointedly that their riches and high standing in society cannot exempt them from it.

In the epistle to Augustus the true poet's devotion to labor and inattention to material things both qualify him as a true Roman and give him his claim to be Augustus's true celebrator against mere flattering amateurs. In the epistle to Florus Horace gives his most explicit and moving account of the emotionally and physically, as well as intellectually, exhausting task. He pictures the composition of poetry as combining the demands made on the attention of a Roman magistrate of the highest rank with the physical demands made on a professional dancer. Only a young poet will be equal to these demands in their full strength. An old poet will have to find different and less exhausting (but not less satisfying) expedients, both in life and in art.

This severe ideal hardly exaggerates the amount of technical labor and learning that went into the formal Latin poetry of all ages from Ennius to Claudian. But the genre allows Horace to soften his presentation of the poetic ideal considerably by humor and irony. In all three poems contrasts to this ideal are drawn, humorously and at length, with the mad poet who hopes to succeed by inspiration and optimism alone, with the mad poems he produces, and with the short life and evil fate of his writings. The looseness and gracefulness of the poems' conversational transitions suggest a freer model for art than the classicism of their explicit precepts at first seems to demand.

The three poems are also united in their attitude to language: they are all meant to encourage a more restricted, purist view of the kind of Latin proper to poetry, especially in the higher genres, than had prevailed under the Republic. Horace is only expressing here a movement in his own time that became the wave of the future; even he and Vergil were regarded by many later poets as sometimes too adventuresome in meter and language. But he is already very unfair to Republican poetry because of it. In the epistle to Augustus and *The Art of Poetry* it is implied at length, and without any really sufficient qualification, that the poets of the Republic had as their chief virtue raw genius without study, that they never blotted a verse. In the epistle to Florus Horace saves his hostility for his contemporaries.

The three poems are still very different pieces, each with its own character. The epistle to Augustus has the clearest and simplest argumentative structure of the three, though it is not without subtle and pregnant "conversational" transitions and spirited ironies, particularly concerning any concept of poetry as mere court flattery. *The Art of Poetry,* as a poem about poems, is on the surface not just conversationally informal but joltingly arbitrary in its succession of topics. Its precepts taken one by one recommend the strictest sort of Aristotelian decorum in art. But it is so audacious and shapeless in its structure and argument that it seems to express more sympathy than one would at first think with the wild formless artwork and the mad poet it condemns with hilarious satire at the beginning and end. The epistle to Florus, which we can examine here as an example of the three, is a sort of middle term: a personal poem, in which the theme of poetics is movingly united with that of self-examination and the loss and gain that come with aging. Through a succession of subtle but never jarring transitions, it builds the most poetically satisfying and unified structure of all Horace's hexameter poems, early or late.

It is the perfect late-Horatian poem, a seamless flow, over easy conversational transitions, of exquisite, autumn-colored verse and valediction. Horace begins with a hilarious picture of a slave dealer selling a native Italian slave boy who is full of beauty and has a talent for literature and song, yet is surprisingly inexpensive. But the slave dealer, to be sure the sale is legal, slips in briefly at the end (in small print, so to speak, and in deliberately ambiguous language) that the slave is apt to wander off and disobey orders.

> "No professional dealer would give you this price. In
>   fact I
> would only do it for you. He did slack off once;
> and as happens, hid out from the hanging whip
>   under the stairs."
> You can give him his money, if "runaway" doesn't
>   hurt you.   [*Epistles* 2.2.13–16]

In law the slave dealer was liable to a lawsuit from the buyer if he left that unmentioned, for even "making himself scarce" against orders, let alone being a runaway (the dealer tries to say this as ambiguously as possible), diminished a slave's price.

"I told you I was lazy when you left," Horace says abruptly (line 20). He is himself the clever hider-out and the tricky slave dealer at once. He told Florus in advance that he was too lazy to write this poem (which he is of course writing: the old joke again), and no lawsuit can lie against him. What sounds like an army story of Horace's youth follows, and another moral is immediately drawn. A soldier in Lucullus's army in the 60s B.C. had his savings stolen by a cutpurse and immediately became the bravest man in the army, conquering one of the enemy King Mithridates' royal citadels single-handed. He was brilliantly rewarded with money. That was the end of his ambition. The next time Lucullus asked for his services in conquering another citadel, he was told: "Someone will go—someone who's lost his wallet" (lines 39–40). Without pause, Horace draws the moral of this story by reviewing his own earlier history. I paraphrase: "I was brought up at Rome and learned there my Homer; Athens

added more to my education; but I went from there into warfare
that did not prevail against Caesar Augustus's might and
power. I came home impoverished and was driven by the au-
dacity of poverty into being a poet. What sort of fool would I be
if I had not rather sleep late than write verse?"

But this sarcastic tone suddenly turns into pathos. Verse is
indeed what he called it in *The Art of Poetry*, an arduous profession worth the efforts of a man's whole lifetime. But Florus does
not appreciate that it is a physical effort, an exhausting one.

> The years rob us of everything as they go by:
> they've taken good-humor and love and banquets and
>   play.
> They want to twist poems away from me: what
>   should I do?   [*Epistles* 2.2.55–57]

To write for the various tastes of the public, to keep up
one's business duties and rounds of social calls in Rome, to
participate in its hypocritical and backbiting literary society—all
these are distracting enough. Horace is being his intentionally
two-faced self here. He means that he has in fact pleased various
publics with his satires, epodes, and odes, that he is still important in Roman business and society, and is still loaded down
with business whenever he visits the city, and that he is still a
major figure in literary society.

But Horace himself dismisses all these "strains" of success
in Rome as superficial. The real reason for his despair of writing
poetry like that of his youth is the strain and anguish of composition, of perpetually correcting, reworking, discarding. His
own exhausting and tiring work at his art he describes under the
metaphor (an unusually extended one) of a censor. In the real
world the censor's responsibility was to revise the rolls of Senate, knights, and people without fear of those he struck out; also
to admit new citizens, whatever their parentage, who seemed
worthy. He supervised building contracts for the beautification
of the city, and enforced sumptuary laws against unnecessary
luxury in dress and dinner giving. But the poet's arduous "magistracy" is exercised over the phantom-world of language. At
the end it collapses into what seems to the public, though not to
the anguished poet, merely the effortless dance of a great mime.

A man who wants to make what is really a poem
takes up with his tablets the soul of a harsh Roman
    censor:
He will not flinch from canceling what is not
    splendid,
what is weightless and flighty, unworthy of high
    place,
from crossing out words, though they seem unwilling
    to go
and plead residence rights in his inmost hearth and
    shrine.
He will also firmly restore words forgotten
by the Roman people, and bring fine words for real
    things
to light that our nobles in Cato's day used
but are now deserted and old and gray with decay.
He'll inscribe new ones whose only parent is Usage.
Then flowing, and clear, and liquid as the full river,
he will pour out wealth and enrich Latium with
    words,
but repress luxuriance, soften all that is harsh
with intelligent pruning, and cast out all that is
    nerveless;
he will appear as if playing and be in real torture: like
    dancers
that must twist to be satyr and Cyclops in the same
    play.   [*Epistles* 2.2. 109–25]

For this effort, Horace says, he is too old; the study of
philosophy and the acceptance of life are more proper. His reputation concerns him less, too, because he is only involved with
what is really and philosophically true about his life (another
anticipation of the modern language of the psychology of aging:
the results Horace attributes to "philosophy" often cross with
those of modern psychology). Horace here seems to glance
around his own large country possessions as he discusses the
avoidance of avarice. Does he own them, or merely have the use
of them, as anyone who bought their produce might be said to
as well? The law gives him their possession in fee simple. But
life and the passage of time tell a different law. Human beings

have only the usufruct of their possessions for life. Nothing is
permanent. Heir follows heir like wave on wave (lines 158–79).

Horace takes his old theme of avarice for the example of his
new style of self-searching because it continues themes in the
poem and because it brings in a new one: the review of life ends
in the thought of death. The sale of the clever runaway slave at
the beginning started a theme of legal imagery which continues
in the long metaphor of the censor and ends in this passage full
of parody references to the Roman law of real property. It also
started the theme of the fugitiveness and impermanence of everything in life, which comes to a climax here: as in the great
lyrics about death, property and the thought of ownership bring
up only the sad thought of the brevity and impermanence of the
owner. This time the prosperous landowner is Horace himself,
and he frees himself as part of his life-review from the illusion of
ownership and possession. His lands are as fugitive as his youth
and his earlier lyric style. A reputable Roman was almost de-
fined by his attention to increasing the family estate during his
lifetime and passing it on to his heirs improved. But that means
nothing to Horace, a bachelor, and doubly not now:

> There's a difference, whether you scatter wealth on
>   the ground
> or, neither in pain at spending nor greedy for more,
> behave as you did when a boy on spring holidays
> and enjoy your brief and pleasant time as you can.
> . . . .
> My sails are taut with no violent following north
>   winds,
> my life is not spent in fighting storms from the South;
> strength, genius, beauty, courage, station, and wealth
> put me low among great men but far above the low.
> "You're no miser: Dismissed." Well then: You're free
>   of this vice,
> are you free of the rest? Is your heart done with
>   empty fame?
> Is it free of the fear of death? Is it free of rage?
> Do you give dream-symbols and magical curses and
>   miracles,

fortune-tellers, ghosts in the night, and witches a
  horselaugh?
Do you number your birthdays with thanks to the
  gods and forgive
your friends, ever milder, more generous, as you
  grow old?
What does it help you to pluck out one thorn of
  many?
If you really cannot live well, give place to the
  experts.
You have had enough pleasure, and eaten and drunk
  enough;
it's your time to leave, before you drink far too much
  more
and the young, more decently horny, laugh and put
  you outdoors.   [*Epistles* 2.2.195–98, 201–16]

Many themes are united and transformed in these apparently simple last lines. Horace, in borrowing from Lucretius and
his own earlier self the image of the satisfied/unsatisfied departing guest in life, adds to it the image of rejection by the young.
The Latin echoes the language of the Old Woman lyrics of *Odes*
1–3; but now it is not Lyce's or Canidia's hideousness that is
satirized, but Horace's own fear of rejection by the young in
love. At last, and more explicitly than in *Odes* 4, he here applies
the same images against himself.

But the image is a hopeful one: the banquet is not all there is
to life. In Lucretius and in his own early satires, the image of
departing satisfied from the banquet had been a figure of speech
for death. Horace here makes it a figure for departing from the
life of lyric poetry and its banquets to a new life and a new style.
Wisdom and self-understanding make it possible to leave the
banquet, as age comes, for something new. If the epistle to
Florus was written before 15 B.C., as seems probable, not only
the epistle to Augustus and the *Carmen saeculare* but the immense new lyric world of the fourth book of odes were still
before Horace.

EPILOGUE

I BEGAN BY SAYING THAT THE REACTIONS OF THE RENAISSANCE
and Baroque writers to Horace's work are more interesting than
those of most eighteenth-century and Victorian writers. If we
take one of Horace's acknowledged masterpieces, ode 1.9,
"Vides ut alta stet nive candidum," and examine the reactions
to it of John Dryden (1631–1700) and William Congreve (1670–
1729), they seem able instantly to find things that today's scholars arrive at also, but in far too much slow-paced prose. Here is a
prose version of the ode:

"You see how deep white Soracte stands piled in snow,
how the forests labor with it, and the rivers stand, stilled with
sharp ice. Dissolve the cold, have the wood heaped generously
on the hearth, and pour forth more generously the four-year-old
Sabine wine, Thaliarchus, from its jar. Leave to the gods the
rest. Once they have laid to rest the winds that war with the
boiling sea, neither the cypresses nor the ancient ash trees tremble. What is to come, do not ask. Whatever day Fortune gives
you, mark up to profit. While you are young, scorn neither love
affairs nor dances, as long as morose grey hairs are absent from
your greenness. Now the parks and the piazzas are yours to
visit at the agreed-on hour, and the soft whispers of the night-
time, now the pleasant laugh that betrays a girl hiding in a secret
corner, and the pledge of love snatched from her arms or a
hardly-resisting finger."

An anthology larger than this book could be made of articles
"proving" or doubting that this is a good poem, in spite of its
apparent confusion of seasons, since Thaliarchus would catch
cold if he stopped pouring wine and followed Horace's advice
"now." In the nineteenth century the great Greek scholar
Wilamowitz, followed since by many and disagreed with by still
more, laid down that "these are pretty verses, but no poem."

("hübsche Verse, aber noch kein Gedicht"). Critical articles protesting that "now" only means "while you are young"—that the winter of the opening lines imagistically suggests old age, and that youth and spring are its natural parallel—and adducing other similar excuses for Horace's daring have now piled up to such a point that Thaliarchus could spare the logs and build a sizable fire from the offprints.

Why did no one need to be told this in the seventeenth century? It is true that the audaciousness of this poem is not "classical" and very hard to parallel in surviving Greek or Latin poetry. It is more like a piece of perfect Zen that one could compare to the poems of great Japanese masters of the haiku and the Noh like Basho and Zeami, to whom the collapsing of seasons and times by pure thought was a familiar theme. We read that Basho once scored over a party of poets who were composing haiku on the subject of the full moon hanging over them. Not knowing who he was (he was in beggar's clothes), they turned to the apparent beggar and condescended to let him compete. "'Lo, the *new* moon,'" he began, and was received with horror and astonishment. But he continued: "I said, and waited. Now I have my surprise." The company instantly recognized a master and led him to the head of the banquet.

Horace probably had no such beautiful acclamation from his audience when he recited this poem, but it seems improbable that any of his contemporaries misunderstood what he was trying to do. Here is Dryden's version of the first part:

> Beyond yon mountain's hoary height
>   Made higher with new mounts of snow;
> Again behold the winter's weight
>   Oppress the labouring woods below
> And streams, with icy fetters bound,
> Benumm'd and crampt to solid ground.
> With well-heaped logs dissolve the cold,
>   And feed the genial hearth with fires;
> Produce the wine, that makes us bold,
>   And sprightly wit and love inspires;
> For what hereafter shall betide,
> God, if 'tis worth his care, provide.

> Let Him alone, with what he made,
>   To toss and turn the world below;
> At His command the storms invade,
>   The winds by his commission blow;
> Till with a nod he bids 'em cease,
> And then the calm returns, and all is peace.

With the words *hoary, benumm'd, crampt*, Dryden simply settles whether the winter is an allegory of old age. The verse-paraphrase of this poem written a decade or two later by the great Restoration dramatist Congreve also takes this allegory for granted; but what I want to quote is his fantasy on the all-important word *now*:

> Seek not to know to morrow's Doom:
> That is not ours, which is to come.
> The present Moment's all our Store;
>   The next, should Heav'n allow,
>   Then this will be no more:
> So all our Life is but one Instant *Now*.
>   Look on each Day you've past
> To be a mighty Treasure won;
> And lay each Moment out in haste;
>   We're sure to live too fast,
>   And cannot live too soon.
> . . . .
> *Now* Love, that everlasting Boy, invites
> To revel, while you may, in soft Delights;
> *Now* the kind Nymph yields all her Charms,
> Nor yields in vain to youthful Arms.

That this word *now* is the secret axis of the mysterious little poem, Congreve simply saw.

This poetic trust that Horace is always doing something alive and interesting started to weaken in the next century. The great writers of the Age of Reason were more cautious about simply giving themselves up to Horace's or anyone else's lyric genius and seeing where it led them. The calmer mode of the *Satires* and *Epistles* was more to their taste: these poems, at least, saved Horace for another hundred years as a liberating model of skepticism and humane good sense in a bigoted and foolish world. Voltaire's "Epistle: To Horace" is only a specially fine example among many:

> J'ai vécu plus que toi; mes vers dureront moins.
> Mais au bord du tombeau je mettrai tous mes soins
> A suivre les leçons de ta philosophie,
> A mépriser la mort en savourant la vie,
> A lire tes écrits pleins de grâce et de sens,
> Comme on boit d'un vin vieux qui rajeunit les sens.
> . . . .
> Tes maximes, tes vers,
> Ton esprit juste et vrai, ton mépris des enfers,
> Tout m'assure qu'Horace est mort en honnête
>   homme.
> Le moindre citoyen mourait ainsi dans Rome;
> Là, jamais on ne vit monsieur l'abbé Grisel
> Ennuyer un malade au nom de l'Eternel.

> I have lived longer than you did; my verses will live less; but here at the edge of the grave I shall set myself wholly to follow the lessons of your philosophy, to spurn death in savoring life, and read your poems full of grace and sense as I would drink old wine to feel young again. . . . Your maxims, your verse, your fair and true spirit, your scorn for the afterlife, all assure me Horace died like an honest man; the least citizen died like that in Rome; one never heard there of M. l'Abbé Grisel boring a sick man in the name of the Eternal.

But here the problems of the modern world with Horace have already started to appear. Even that heartfelt tribute to Horace as an incarnation of Roman spiritual freedom does not go deep enough. Voltaire himself wants too much to appropriate Horace, to make Horace agree with his own Age of Reason skepticism. In reality the attraction and challenge of reading Horace should be greater than that. It comes from his being no more usable as a prop for Voltaire's own personal ideology, or anyone else's, than for its opposite: the antipathy between Horace and dogma goes deeper than Voltaire saw.

After the Baroque era not much represents to me as brilliantly as Ariosto's or Wyatt's or Dryden's Horatian "voices" the sort of poet I have tried to describe in this book. No Greek or Roman poet seems to have been more the prisoner of his own tradition in recent times. In Horace's case, this is the tradition of "Horatian" poetry that grew up from 1700 to 1900. Pope's versions of and allusions to the *Satires* and *Epistles* recreate their originals as admirably in English as Boileau's earlier ones do in French, and Samuel Johnson's version of *Odes* 4.7 is not the only eighteenth- or nineteenth-century poem in English or other languages that shows a feeling for the hardness and terror that lurks beneath the bright surface of the lyric poems. And certainly Horace has always had adorers, even in ages where this adoration could only find what seems today pedantic or superficial expression. One cannot speak with utter contempt of the Victorian tradition without remembering innumerable insights still to be gained from nineteenth-century commentaries in English, French, and German. The peasants around Vicovaro and in the valley of the Digentia, where the Sabine farm was, are said to have labored throughout the nineteenth century under the impression that Horace was an Englishman, so many pilgrims from that country appeared there every year. Still, Marvell's "Horatian Ode," and some of the Horatian paraphrases by his contemporary Abraham Cowley, seem to me to be among the last English poems of any distinction that invoke Horace; they antecede the biographical and personal tradition that the eighteenth and nineteenth centuries created around Horace, and are an unprejudiced reaction to the poems themselves. After that, we have only flareups of the true reaction of poets to Horace as another poet. What is professedly "Horatian" in poetry seldom fails to be deadened and spoiled by the textbook biography, the expectation of indifferentism and affected bachelor serenity.

Horace's influence on other poets in antiquity was exactly like his influence on the poets of the Renaissance and Baroque. Persius's famous lines about Horace as satirist convey a sense of his elusive ambiguity rather than his modest personality: "Every vice clever Horace touches, but as a friend who keeps smiling and, having once got into you, plays—but round the very heartstrings" Persius 1.116f.). Juvenal seems unaware that his satire is not "Horatian." Seneca never read a biography of Horace as a patron of squirely mediocrity, and neither did Boethius, nor would either have believed it. That is because as Romans themselves they appreciated the Roman realities of his poems. There is no "Horatian" contentment in a word they write: Seneca's violent tragedies and Boethius's stern *Consolatio* are just full, and gloriously full, of echoes of Horace's poetry.

Horace is best taken, then, apart from any expectations that the literary category of the "Horatian" may still arouse. He deserves to be studied as a great Italian artist of a period of change and transition in his country's history, no differently from the way one would approach Raphael or Titian. The techniques that have done most for him in this century's criticism sound merely academic, but turn out to have profound human meaning. Study of Roman social history has been very profitable in abolishing the old notion that Horace's circle of lovers and friends is a literary creation, or that his poems were not immediately relevant to their addressees: something real and drawn from experience is always worked into the literary model he draws on to give it life. Appreciation of the position that Horace and people like him really held in Roman society dissolves what was once taken for humility into an opaquely polite governing-class pose. As history turns from the study of great persons to the study of their society as a whole, Horace's developing relation to Augustus and Rome, year by year of his life, has come to seem immensely more complex and positive than a mere change from Brutus and "liberty" to uncomfortable praise of monarchy.

So also the literary critical techniques that have helped most to keep Horace alive in this century are New Criticism; the study of the unity of the Augustan poetry book; and the redefining of Horace's self-portrait as an artistic creation, a persona, only very subtly related to biographical reality. These sound merely literary at first, merely academic, but they make profoundly human points about Horace. They focus attention where it belongs, on the poetry, and help restore him to his proper place among artists. New Criticism is only the justification of Horace's own statement that he labored all his life for a simplicity that cost him blood, and would cost anyone else blood to imitate. It demonstrates the endless implications and echoes behind his simple words. The good comments on, and interesting critical reactions to, his poems can be as endless as their readers. The concept of the Augustan poetry book raises still further our valuation of Horace's intelligence and ability to combine complex ideas (though perhaps it is no great compliment to our modern understanding that it took us so long to trust Horace and his contemporaries to remember ten or twenty of their own poems at once and consider the whole effect their arrangement in order would make as a whole).

The concept of the poetic persona has a historical as well as a literary integrity. It reminds a reader how little, particularly in the later poems, Horace tells about the events of his own life, for all his air of confiding in the reader as a familiar friend; and how fully his poems take advantage of the irony of literature itself to represent the ambiguities and ironies of all human thoughts. Charles Brink calls him "one of the clearest intelligences in the history of Western poetry," and like Bowra's startling remark about the range of experience presented in the *Odes*, that may seem at first an unexpected and extravagant compliment. Is this not the language in which one would speak of Lucretius or Dante? But the longer one studies Horace the truer it seems. The poetry itself first suggests, then evaporates by its ironies, the familiar portrait. The persevering reader is left alone with a pure, cold intelligence involved in a battle with human commitment, emotion, and the sense of community, the only things for which it is at all willing to compromise its integrity. The model Horace's poetry leaves for that struggle is one that centuries of readers have found inexhaustible.

BIBLIOGRAPHICAL NOTE
AND ACKNOWLEDGMENTS

THIS BRIEF BIBLIOGRAPHICAL NOTE IS MEANT FOR READERS WHO ARE NOT professional students of the classics, but would like to read further in and about Horace. "Good" translations of Horace are mostly called so by courtesy, and many times in making my own for this book I have had to console myself with the old saw that a translator of Horace into English is making ropes out of sand. That understood, several good paperback translations are easily available, and a reader of Horace should own several. Joseph Clancy's older version of the *Odes* and *Epodes* (Chicago, 1960) is not quite superseded by W. G. Shepherd's Penguin translation (Harmondsworth, 1983), good as that is, and some odes are still best translated for the modern reader by James Michie, whose version with facing Latin (New York, 1963) is now out of print, but available in most libraries. Smith Palmer Bovie's version of the *Satires* and *Epistles* (Chicago, 1962) is still worth having, even though the notes and commentary in Niall Rudd's Penguin version (Harmondsworth, 1973) are much superior. There is a very fine translation of the *Epistles* by Colin MacLeod (Rome, 1986). Also, there are interesting translations of many key poems, both hexameter and lyric, in Burton Raffel's *Essential Horace* (San Francisco, 1983).

For those who have some Latin and who would like to return to Horace in the original, the two-volume Loeb Classical Library edition is good enough in the *Satires* and *Epistles* (Cambridge, Mass., and London, 1929), but not very distinguished in its treatment of the *Odes* and *Epodes* (1934). A helpful supplement, which is in many libraries, is the old Victorian crib, Clarke's *Interlinear Horace*. Gordon Williams's *Third Book of Horace's Odes* (Oxford, 1969), with Latin text, English translation, and thorough, interesting commentary, is more useful by far; more of Horace ought to be available in this format or a similar one. There are two general biographies and surveys of Horace's work, by J. Perret (trans. B. Humez, New York, 1964) and Kenneth Reckford (in the Twayne World Authors series, New York, 1969). Both, like this book, are simply titled *Horace*, and both are well worth reading (Perret more for historical background and information, Reckford more for literary criticism and appreciation).

As for more detailed studies: on the *Odes*, the standard books in English for the nonspecialist reader are still Steele Commager's *Odes of Horace* (New Haven, 1962) and L. P. Wilkinson's *Horace and His Lyric Poetry* (Cambridge, 1946), both full of fine things. For my view that the *Odes* as well as the *Epistles* and *Satires* are arranged into well-designed books that progress in thought, I am indebted (among others) to Matthew Santirocco, *Unity and Design in Horace's* Odes (Chapel Hill, 1986). On the *Satires*, there are Niall Rudd's *Satires of Horace* (Cambridge, 1966) and the essays in W. S. Anderson's *Essays in Roman Satire* (Princeton, 1982); on *Epistles* 1, Ross Kilpatrick, *The Poetry of Friendship* (Edmonton, 1986). A nonclassicist reader who wants to know more about Horace's historical period should consult Donald Earl's *Age of Augustus* (New York and London, 1968), a book whose pictorial presentation of Augustus's world and its immense remaining monuments is as remarkable as its fair-minded estimation of Augustus's political achievement; also, Jasper Griffin's *Augustan Poetry and Roman Life* (Oxford, 1985), a delightfully lively account of the real world to which Horace's poetry alludes. There are also good further essays for the general reader in David West's *Reading Horace* (Edinburgh, 1967), in C. D. N. Costa's collection *Horace* (London, 1973), and in David West and Tony Woodman's three anthologies *Quality and Pleasure in Latin Poetry* (Cambridge, 1974), *Creative Imitation and Latin Literature* (Cambridge, 1979), and *Poetry and Politics in the Age of Augustus* (Cambridge, 1984). As is the way of classical scholarship, the bibliographies of the books mentioned in this paragraph lead on to further reading at any length and level one has time for.

I myself am indebted to all these authors and many more I cannot acknowledge here. But I may and must also acknowledge some special debts I incurred in writing this book. First and foremost, to the editor of this series, a master of English style and expression no less than of scholarship, whose patient, detailed, and helpful reading of successive drafts reminded me continually of Horace's own characterization of the good critic (*The Art of Poetry* 436–51). So also I owe a great deal to the detailed criticisms, literary, historical, and stylistic, of my colleague M. Gwyn Morgan; and to some friends without, or without professional-level, Latin or Greek, but with much literary sensitivity, especially J. D. M. Dunne and Mark Toles, who read the manuscript for me to clear out any pedantry that a nonclassicist might find opaque. Any that remains is no more their fault than any errors of fact or expression that remain are the editor's. Where I have simply agreed with a previous interpretation, as with Nisbet's of epode 9, Reckford's of ode 4.6, West's of ode 1.7 or 3.4, it did not seem relevant to the plan of this series to indicate that with a note. But three special presents made me personally by other scholars I can acknowledge with special gratitude. My analysis of the fourth book of *Odes* as a whole started from some hints in an article on ode 4.1 by Thomas Habinek, "The Marriageability of Maximus" (*American Journal of Philosophy* 107 [1986]:407–16). Professor Habinek was good enough to encourage me to develop these as I liked for this book; of course, he is not responsible for the details of this exposition or for the brief venture into the poetics of the Noh play with which I try to justify it. I could never have developed my exposition of *Epistles* 1 (particularly of what I call the "doxographical" theme) without the help given me over decades of discussion of Horace by a friend of thirty years' standing, Michael Wigodsky. I have also profited more than I can say from the detailed suggestions of another long-time friend, William Kupersmith, a great scholar of the Horatian tradition in English literature (I wish I had been able to satisfy him by making my comments on that tradition less brief and unsubtle). The great poet of friendship is almost as strong a bond between people who like him as friendship itself.

INDEX

Aelius Stilo Praeconinus, L., 11
Agrippa, M. Vipsanius, 68, 73, 95
Alcaeus: as model for Horatian
    lyric, 68, 82
Alcaic meter, 74–75
Anacreon, 82
Antony, Mark, 15–16, 19, 47, 68,
    87–88, 91, 142
Antonius, Iullus, 142
Aratus, 101
Archilochus, 56
Arius Didymus (Augustan dox-
    ographer), 118
Asclepiadean meters, 68, 75–76
Athens, in the late Roman Re-
    public, 13–16
Augustus: as Octavian, 15, 19;
    less prominent than Maecenas
    in Horace's earlier poems, 20–
    21, 47, 63–64; as patron in Odes
    1–3, 66–67, 68, 77, 93–106, 112,
    115; Horace's irony towards, in
    Odes 2.9 and 2.12, 98–99; in
    3.14, 105–06; in 3.29, 112; in
    Epistles 1.16, 129–31; greater ac-
    ceptance of his regime in
    Horace's later poems, 135–36,
    145, 150–53, 154–55; made
    Horace's heir, 153–54

Bacchylides, 68; as source for an
    epithet in Odes 3.26, 84
Basho, 164
Boethius, 168
Bowra, Maurice, 115

Brink, Charles, 169
Brophy, Brigid: on the "Hora-
    tian" in poetry, 6
Brutus, M. Junius, 8, 9, 15–18,
    89, 168

Callimachus: as model for the
    "Hellenistic" elements in Hora-
    tian style, 35, 42, 50, 65, 156
Catullus, 56, 61, 68
Censores, 13, 155–56, 159–60
Cicero, 14
Coactores, 11
Congreve, William: as translator
    and critic of Odes 1.9, 163–65

Dellius, Q., 90–91
"Diatribe" form in relation to sat-
    ire, 28–30
Doxography and doxographers,
    117–18
Drusus, Nero Claudius: conquest
    of Rhaetia, 142–44, 151
Dryden, John: on "Horatian" and
    "Juvenalian" satire, 6n; as
    translator of Odes 3.29, 110–11;
    as translator and critic of Odes
    1.9, 163–65

Epictetus, 139
Euripides: Bacchae imitated in
    Odes 2.19 and Epistles 1.16, 113,
    129–30

Freedmen, status of, 10–12, 14–
    15
Freedwomen, 34

Goethe, J. W. von, 148

Hesoid, 103
Hipponax, 56
Horace: early life, 9–11; ambi-
    tions for senatorial rank, 13–14;
    education in Athens, 14; with
    Brutus at Philippi, 15–18; at-
    tains equestrian rank, 15, 18–
    19; during Second Triumvirate
    (41–31 B.C.), 18–20; friendship
    with Maecenas, 20–25; rela-
    tions with Maecenas and Au-
    gustus in later life, 135–36,
    153–54; death, 153–54
—poetic techniques: use of "Au-
    gustan poetry book" form for
    arranging poems, 26–28, 41–
    47, 48–50, 117–22, 133–34,
    138–53; apolitical nature of sat-
    ire and invective, 27–56; letter-
    and sound-play, 43–44, 90;
    meters of Epodes and lyrics, 55,
    56, 74–76; vocabulary and
    word placement, 69–70, 73–74;
    realism and contemporary de-
    tail in his lyrics, 71–73, 77–80
—poetic themes: bisexuality, 21,
    65–66, 82, 140–41, 148–49; fam-
    ily life and Augustan moral
    legislation, 24–25, 99–101, 114–
    16, 136, 139–41, 152–53; ava-
    rice, 28–32, 42–43, 58–60, 90,
    160–62; friendship and amicitia,
    36–41, 56–58, 119–24, 131–33;
    literary criticism, 41–47, 56,
    133–34, 154–60; the Sabine
    farm, 48–53, 108–12, 118, 119–
    21, 124–29; urbs-rus antithesis,
    58–60; aging, 60–61, 67, 83–84,
    122, 138–41, 145–46, 147–50,

160–62; older women as sym-
    bols of rejection in love, 60–63,
    83–84; Roman politics, 63–65,
    134–39; love, 65–66, 76–87,
    140–41, 148–50; self-praise as
    poet, 70–73, 115–16, 133–35,
    142; maps and geographical
    themes, 73, 102–03, 111, 118,
    137, 142–44, 151; Rome and
    contemporary Greeks, 78–80,
    97; Campus Martius as scene
    for love poetry, 80–83; wealth
    and death, 87–93, 119–24, 131–
    33, 160–62; Augustus as patron
    of state poetry, 93–106; Di-
    onysus as symbol of poetic and
    philosophical independence,
    94, 113–14, 129–31; pre-
    cariousness of Augustan re-
    gime in 23 B.C. reflected in
    Odes 1–3, 94–106; stability of
    Augustan regime reflected in
    later lyrics, 136–38; older wom-
    en in later poetry, 149–50, 162
"Horatian" as literary category,
    x, 5–6, 8–9
Horatius, the elder (Horace's fa-
    ther), 2–4, 10–16, 24, 44

Jonson, Ben, 48, 140–41
Julius Caesar, 13, 15–16
Juvenal, 6, 27, 28, 168
"Juvenalian" as literary category,
    5–6, 168

Lucilius: as "classical" model for
    Horatian satire, 26–27, 29, 35;
    Horace's literary criticism of,
    41–44, 45–47, 56
Lucretius: compared with Horace
    as influence in literary history,
    5; topos about lovers applied to
    friendship in Horace, 39; on so-
    cial contract, 40; topos of the
    satisfied guest in Lucretius and
    Horace, 32, 162

Maecenas: as Horace's patron
    and friend in youth, 20–25;
    characterized by Seneca, 21, 22;
    quoted, 22; in the *Satires*, 27,
    28, 30, 33, 37–41, 45, 47, 53–55;
    in the *Epodes*, 56–58, 65; in the
    Odes, 70–73, 77, 98–99; ten-
    sions with Augustus at period
    of *Odes 1–3*, 95–96, 106–11; in
    Horace's later poems, 119–24,
    133–34, 149; relations with
    Horace in later life, 135–36, 153
Marcellus, M. Claudius, 95–96
Messalla, M. Valerius, 16, 18, 47,
    87
Munatius Plancus, L., 87–89, 95,
    106, 115

Nietzsche, Friedrich, 69

Orbilius of Beneventum, 12

Persius, 167–68
Philodemus of Gadara, 35–36,
    78–79, 80, 82
Pindar, 68, 96, 102; *Pythian 1* as
    model for *Odes 3.4*, 104–05; as
    reference point and model in
    Odes 4, 142–44
Plato, 39; *Phaedrus* as source for
    Odes 2.20, 72; *Symposium* as
    source for *Epistles 1.16*, 130
Pope, Alexander, 31, 167
Praecones, 11

Roman Odes (*Odes 3.1–6*), 99–105
Rudd, Niall, 6n

Sanderson, Robert, 74
Sapphic meter, 68, 74–75
Sappho, 68, 82
Scribae quaestorii, 18
Seneca, 21, 22, 168
Sestius, L., 89–90
Social War (*91–87* B.C.), 9–10
Spartacus, 10
Statius, 69
Stendhal, 24
Stesichorus, 61
Strabo, 80

Tennyson, Alfred, 75
Tiberius Claudius Nero: in
    Epistles 1, 118; conquest of
    Rhaetia, 142–44, 151
Tribuni militum, 15
Terence, 3–4

Ueda, Makoto, 137–38

Varro Murena, Licinius, 6, 105–
    08
Venusia, 9–12, 18, 113
Vergil: introduces Horace to
    Maecenas, 20; in Maecenas's
    Symposium, 22, 59–60; *Aeneid* as
    reference point in *Odes 4*, 144,
    146–47, 152
Voltaire, 166

Zeami Motokiyo, 137–38, 164